An American Nomad

An American Nomad

A Road Trip in Search of America

Stephen Braxton Thompson

An American Nomad
A Road Trip in Search of America

v5.0

Outskirts Press, Inc.
http://www.outskirtspress.com

ISBN: 978-1-4327-9802-4

PRINTED IN THE UNITED STATES OF AMERICA

To Hunter, my eldest grandson,
who taught us a lesson in courage...

In memory of Ketty,
for whom it ended far too soon,

&

Bill Latch

Neil Chafin, Supang Povatong, and Jack Fleischer

To Chris Chafin —

All the very best!

D. B. [illegible]

6/8/13

Don't cry because it's over. Smile because it happened.

~Dr. Seuss

Acknowledgments

If I wore a hat, I'd tip it to *Mazda* for making an automobile as rock solid as the little blue hatchback which tagged along with me on my year-long journey around the USA. I can't overlook *Goodyear* for the rubber which kept me connected to the road; *Priceline* for its help booking inexpensive accommodations along the way; *Google* for online maps and research tools; *Coppertone* for its sunscreen products; *Denny's* for hearty breakfasts; *LL Bean* for rugged clothing; *The Coin Laundry Association,* whose membership allowed me to wear clean socks and underwear from time to time; *National Public Radio* for keeping me informed; *The Weather Channel* for guiding me out of harm's way...most of the time; *Dollar General* for a steady supply of inexpensive reading glasses, which I tend to lose or sit on at every available opportunity; *Frito-Lay* for the *Cheetos*; *Nexium* for controlling the heartburn one inevitably encounters on the road eating at truck stops, fast food restaurants, mall food courts, carnivals, convenience stores, and hot dog stands; *Sunsweet Prune Juice* for helping me maintain an even keel; *Raid* for its flying insect killer; Bill Gates for *Windows*; John Gorrie for inventing the ice cube; the inventor of GPS, Bradford Parkinson; *Walgreen's* for toiletries and medications; my son for the *snake gaiters*; *Netflix* for its *Watch Instantly* feature; Bob Dylan, the Rolling Stones, Bruce Springsteen, Simon & Garfunkel, Dusty Springfield, Jimmy

Buffett, Bee Gees, Deborah Harry, Tom Petty, Judy Collins, Rod Stewart, Willie Nelson, Luciano Pavarotti, The Drifters, The Beach Boys, The Lettermen, Celtic Woman, Neil Diamond, Tom Waits, Barbra Streisand, Temptations, and Bob Seger for the *beat*; God for the dawns and sunsets; the U.S. National Park Service and Federal Recreational Lands for its ten dollar *Lifetime Senior Pass*; local, state, and national Park Rangers, employees and volunteers for their invaluable assistance every mile of the way; and all those people across our great land who took time out of their busy lives to spend a few moments with me.

Special gratitude goes to my parents—Jessie and Clary—for giving me life, love, an appreciation for distant horizons, along with making sure I always had plenty to eat and great Christmas presents; my siblings—Richard and Dede—for always being there for me, even when I was a terrible person, which was often; my three children—Charlotte, Amy, and Ben—for giving true meaning to my life, and for not moving in with me after college; my six grandchildren who'll carry my genetic code into the future; Alan A. for the heads-up; Bernie and Wayman, guys who went way out on a professional limb for me; Cindy and Janie for looking after me when I was far from home and feeling very much alone; dedicated bureau staffers who made it all possible: My Binh, P.T., Supang, Sumontha, Phaibool, Boonchoi, Mariko, and Delia; The Foreign Correspondent's Club of Thailand; my book rep, Deni; Cindy K. for pointing the way; Deborah C. for taking my calls at all hours; T.R. for the taste of what I'd missed; L.L. for the very good year; L.M. for easing the transition back to *civilization*; Laurin S. for keeping an eye on my mom; Beth for the family ties; remembering cousin Kay who lovingly documented the long history of the Thompson's in the Sandhills of North Carolina; cousins Sue and David for filling in some blanks; Jessie M. for the first gallery show; the WSSU Class of '94; the men and woman of *Falls Church Fire and Rescue*; the ER staff at *Inova Alexandria*; Doctors Andersen, Varney, and Mushtaq; the Fleischer, Blanchy, and Guedes clans; a little kid named Leo who allowed me one last chance to get parenthood *nearly* right; Ana for the roof and nursing me back to health after a far too close encounter with eternity; my two former wives for bearing my children and at least finding *something* about me they liked in the beginning...and I certainly can't fail to mention all those ultimately disappointed women passing in and out of my life over the years who somehow resisted the temptation to shoot me.

Introduction

I became a journalist because one guy died...and another liked my tie.

The year was nineteen sixty-eight. I had law school in my crosshairs when a casual acquaintance who sat beside me in some long since forgotten university class told me there was an immediate opening for an evening shift street reporter at the local NBC television affiliate where he worked and that I should seriously consider applying for the job.

Now, I'm not at all sure why he even brought it up. It's possible I'd mentioned to him in passing I was looking for something to bring in a little extra cash until law school started that fall, but television news reporter certainly wasn't on my radar screen. I was thinking more in terms of positions for which I was clearly far better suited—like waiter, grocery store stock boy, or maybe even a night watchman.

The TV job opened up when a reporter at the station dropped dead the night before. Of what I don't remember, if I ever knew in the first place, or if I even bothered asking. What I did know, and remember, is I needed money badly and if landing a decent job meant stepping over the still warm body of the recently departed, so be it.

I was married, barely twenty-four, my firstborn was approaching three and her sister would soon be on the way. Our parents and student loans were propping us up financially while I finished school, so money was always very tight.

The general game plan was any job I took would be a short-term proposition to enable us to enjoy a few *luxuries*—like eating meat once a week—as well as put away a little money for a rainy day, although I couldn't imagine it raining any harder than it already was.

I knew I didn't have a chance in hell of getting the job, but figured there'd be no harm done if I went in for an interview. Not only would I get to see the inner workings of an actual television station, an exciting prospect, but could also inquire if the station needed a night watchman.

I was flabbergasted when I was hired on the spot. It made no sense on any level. Still doesn't. I had zero experience, wasn't photogenic, didn't come close to being gifted with a rich TV voice, my hair was longish and unruly, and I favored bell bottoms and brightly-colored shirts with impossibly large collars. Little doubt I was a child of the mildly rebellious side of the late-sixties and not one of those well-groomed, buttoned-down types I saw delivering the news on television in such irritatingly mellifluous tones.

As it turned out, none of that seemingly mattered. The green paisley tie I wore to the job interview sealed the deal. The thirty-something news director admired the tie, I gave it to him, and he gave me the job. Just like that. The entire process took maybe five minutes. I kid you not.

I never did make it to law school, of course, and remain in the dark to this very day why I was really hired, but never asked because I decided it would be unwise to draw attention to the multitude of compelling reasons why I shouldn't have been hired in the first place.

And so began my career in broadcast journalism.

One week after coming onboard, there I was standing in front of a television camera, terrified and totally clueless, but I somehow managed to bullshit my way through my rookie season without making too big a fool of myself, although there were times I saw the poor news director banging his head against a wall.

I won't bore you with details, but eventually—and God only knows how *this* happened—I somehow managed to ascend the broadcast news ladder, and before I knew it I was winging off to my very first war. Six years had passed since I was the most unlikely of hires, and I was still scratching my head over the way life had turned out, even as my international flight touched down at Saigon's Ton Son Nhut Airport.

I'm not exactly sure *what* I had in mind in the early stages of considering writing an actual book. The most logical course would have been to recount in chronological order my years as a journalist, but the memoir market was already flooded with sparkling literary endeavors by former colleagues, most with careers far more interesting and diverse than mine, and there was very little, if anything, I would be able to contribute to the already saturated conversation.

I wanted to do something different, even at the very real risk of falling flat on my face. It wasn't until the idea of a cookie-cutter memoir collided head-on with budding plans to challenge myself with a long road trip around the USA that it all began to come together in my head. Simply stated, I'd attempt to meld select elements of the two disparate subjects under a single umbrella and see where it led, if anywhere.

The road trip pretty much sprang to life out of pure boredom, along with the sobering realization that after all that time living overseas, and languishing year after year *inside* Washington's Capital Beltway, I knew distressingly little of what lay over the American horizon. Those deserts, canyons, forests, rivers, mountains, and remote peopled enclaves were strangers to me, and me to them, so the decision was made to shelve the common conception of a comfortable retirement—in my case, a townhouse on a golf course in a resort community in North Carolina—and hit the road again, determined to learn all I could about the land of my birth...how people live, what they think, the nuances, rhythms and moods which drive, challenge, and sustain the American dream.

A road trip was pretty much a natural for someone like me, I suppose. I'm a nomad at heart. As a youngster, I couldn't sit still for more than a few minutes, and was always off exploring this and that. My father was forever stoking the fire inside me with gifts of books of grand adventures, and he irreparably set my course in life when he joined the diplomatic service when I was six. I was on the move as a kid, rootless and unanchored, blowing from place to place, forever hooked on distant and uncharted places.

I just thank my stars I was able to draw breath in interesting times, had the opportunities I did, and that good luck somehow managed to make its way to my corner when it really mattered. I lay no claim to great accomplishments in life. I made no lasting mark. I won't be remembered. And while I deeply regret the personal missteps and mourn the lost opportunities—there were many and they cut painfully deep—I'm generally okay with the way it all turned out. I pretty much lived life on my own terms, on a global canvas, occupying a prized front row seat to the drama unfolding around me.

-I-

The Mekong Delta. Nineteen Seventy-Five

The morning air is so thick and heavy I can feel my body slicing through it. Not a good day for a walk, but I'm not going all that far. Just to the other side of the rice paddy where the dead litter the ground.

The earth is baked white by the sun and scoured by the wind. The short stubble crunches and snaps under my feet, the heat gathering force, flexing, even at this early hour. It's been a while since rice was harvested in this paddy, or anyone lived in the torched village just off to the right.

I'm closing ground on one particular guy who's caught my eye. No question he's dead. I have zero experience documenting such things, but it's pretty clear to me the man was *fucked*. Beyond *fucked*, actually. I can see all that from hallway across the paddy, even squinting into a glowering tropical sun.

I have no choice now but to suck it up and move in close, really close. Close is where it happens. Close is what it's all about. Close is what I do. And if it bothers me, tough shit. If I can't handle it, then find some other way to earn a living. It's that basic a proposition.

The press on this helicoptered *cluster-fuck* into the Mekong Delta numbers about thirty. A diverse cast of writers and photographers thrown together for the next few hours, but with a common goal—*score* the story and don't *screw the pooch* by getting *wasted*. Getting the hell out of *Dodge* in one piece is priority number one for each and every journalist in each and every combat situation. There are *no* exceptions to this rule. None.

My travel companions include a middle-age, balding French guy slumped down and half asleep, oblivious to the fact he's been scratching his balls with admirable dedication for the past twenty minutes. He's lumped in with an international cross-section of seasoned and *newbie* wire service, newspaper, magazine, and broadcast reporters. All competent professionally, but still pretty much garden variety and languishing on the second tier of their chosen profession. Then there's the group of free-lance photographers, mostly Americans, each focused on snapping an image of such epic magnitude this day it will command a sum of cash on the open market sufficient to allow closing the gap with long overdue bar tabs.

No journalistic *big guns* are to be found on this minor league excursion. They know shit when they smell it.

The two helicopters in our caravan put down on the edge of the rice paddy. A squad of South Vietnamese soldiers in the lead machine immediately fans out and set up a defense perimeter, most scurrying up a steep bank and forming a line along a stream fronting a stand of trees one hundred yards away. If there's trouble, it'll likely come from there.

While I'm slack-jawed at the field of cadavers, for the seasoned photographer's it's a walk in the park. Just checking their gear, chatting about nothing in particular. I wonder if I would ever get to *that* stage. Suspect I would given time. Just the nature of the business. Not exactly something to look forward to, however. My compassion, ability to empathize, is important to me, but it sure as hell didn't take long out here for me to realize I'd have to park chunks of myself from time to time if I want to prosper professionally. Just the price of admission.

I hook up with two of the photographers, both at the doorstep of thirty, like me, and all but joined at the hip. They've been in-country since late sixty-seven. Met during the Tet Offensive a few months later. Learned hard lessons about war, and life, during the week they were pinned down at Khe Sanh. Stayed on in Vietnam after U.S. troops pulled out. Just hanging on now, hoping for one last big score before the communists roll in and they face the prospect of being sucked back into a world which is unkind to those who contribute little beyond excelling at framing photographs of the dead.

There's no doubt the pair's good at what they do. Understood they'd garnered a couple of Pulitzer nominations between them along the way, making them hot commodities with the photo agencies back home when the war was going full tilt. Not bad for a couple of college dropouts who'd arrived in Saigon with second-hand *Nikons* and dreams of adventure, fame and fortune. They'd heard all the stories back home. You can pretty much do as you like in 'Nam. Smoke, snort, bang till you drop. Like "fucking mice" they were soon bragging to envious boyhood friends back home.

They didn't start out this way, of course. A thousand years ago they were All-American kids, going to proms, eating cheeseburgers at the Drive-In, but war did a number on them and there was no going back now, not that they would if they could.

This pair heads for the thickest cluster of corpses, with me in tow. I wasn't invited, but I'm there anyway, two steps behind. These guys know their shit and I don't. Hanging with them seems to be the smart move, but then again I could be sticking my dick in it. No way to know such things for sure. Way too green for that.

The break-in period for a war correspondent is a delicate

proposition, and no allowances are made for stupidity. Look and listen, I'm told. Don't even dare think you have a clue because you don't, and if you step out of line you're probably *toast.*

By the time we reach the far side of the rice paddy I've sweated through my shirt and my hair's all over the place. Mouth's dry, stomach hollow. Trying to muster the courage to do this. About to pop my war zone *cherry.* Just hope I don't screw it up too badly, especially in full view of these guys. Time to suck it up and get down to business.

Just when I think it can't get any worse, it does.

The corpse I'd set my sights on is not that of a man, as I thought, but a boy, maybe twelve or thirteen. The poor kid's been carved up pretty good, riddled from knee to throat by God knows what. Possibly a strafing run by a helicopter gunship. Whatever it was, it was effective.

The boy's rail thin, effeminate with small hands and feet, soft facial features (what's left of them), and bang haircut. He's flat on his back, legs and arms spread apart about as far as possible. His shattered chin tilts towards the right shoulder. He's barefoot, but I spot a single rubber sandal nearby. Blown right out of his shoes, I'd bet. Clutched in his left hand a bent pair of wire eyeglasses. An old rifle with a splintered stock is nearby.

I'd heard about things like this before. Children plucked from their villages by the Viet Cong, brainwashed, given minimal military training, and then unleashed to kill, and be killed. Usually the latter.

This is not fresh meat, but that's not always so easy to determine in the tropics where the raucous heat and humidity tend to accelerate the decomposition process. The bloating carcass is being worked over by assorted squirming creatures. Most congregate in the abundant seeping wounds, and around the gaping mouth and eye sockets. Large, foul-tempered birds are close by, hopping along the ground, flapping their wings and hissing, impatient for me to clear out so they can take *their* turn at the dinner table. Nature is very efficient at sweeping the earth of our mortal remains when we have nothing left to offer.

I battle the urge to throw up. Will it back down as it pushes up. I'm adamant it will not happen. I'll choke to death first. The photographers see my struggle and one walks over.

"Hey, buddy, it's okay to puke. It's no fucking big deal. We all did it when we first got out here. Some pretty mean shit we have to deal with."

"I'll be fine," I mumble. I'm embarrassed, but appreciative of the concern.

"It'll get easier," he says. "They'll come a time when you'll breeze through something like this. Besides, this'll harden you up fast for what's coming, and it's coming, trust me."

Not much comforting about that statement, but suspect it's true.

I'd choppered into the Mekong Delta on a quick in-out expedition organized by South Vietnamese Army in a half-ass, transparent, and pathetic attempt by a doomed regime to convince the world press, and probably itself, it still could counter-punch. Delusional, but it gave me an opportunity to get out of Saigon for a few hours. For that I was grateful.

I'd been lobbying my boss hard for a break from the tedium of being chained to a typewriter and telephone in the Saigon Bureau, fact-finding for the senior correspondents who got all the air time and kudos, while I remained faceless and nameless, and pretty much limited exposure-wise to a few off-hour radio feeds, if I were lucky. As junior staffer I was languishing at the tail end of the food chain and chafing at my situation. I'd been in Saigon for a few months now. A prize assignment for a young reporter anxious to showcase his wares. War zones made careers, but it couldn't be made sitting behind a desk. One had to get out there and run the hazards. Getting some actual field exposure was the ticket to the next level.

As it ultimately played out, I became quite comfortable with the radio side of things. Plenty of opportunity for creativity, and the freedom to function in the field pretty much on my own was certainly appealing and dovetailed neatly with my personality. I'd found my niche, and there I pretty much stayed for the next quarter century.

As we walk back to the helicopters, a shot rings out. Not close, but not far. The Vietnamese Army captain commanding this expedition orders us to get moving. He doesn't have to ask twice.

Snipers scare the hell out of me. Just something about a bullet streaking at me out of the blue. All so impersonal, unfair, and mean-spirited.

A sniper had snuffed out the life of my cousin Tommy in Vietnam eight years earlier up in the Central Highlands. Tommy was a big, awkward kid. A really sweet guy. Not a bad bone in his body. Drove a newspaper delivery truck in civilian life back in North Carolina. As the war heated up, he'd volunteered to serve in the military for all the right reasons.

Tommy stood six-five and weighed around two hundred forty, putting him pretty much head and shoulders above everyone in his platoon, and this was probably what got him killed. The sniper saw this supersize American standing there, an inviting target, and uncorked one. The bullet struck Tommy between the eyes and all but decapitated him. Tommy was twenty-two years old.

The company commander wrote Tommy's mother her son was dead before he hit the ground, as if knowing he never suffered would make all that much of a difference. Maybe it did. I hope so. Aunt Virginia never talked about it during the remaining years of her life, but Uncle Howard told me she often cried herself to sleep.

I learned quickly out on the front lines there's a world of hurt anxious to bring you down. Some of it physical, some emotional. Either way it cuts to the quick. When it's raining down, you question every decision you ever made which led you to that precise spot at that precise moment in time.

While I've never really been all that afraid of *death*, the process of *dying* is quite something else, especially if it involves ghastly wounds, the spilling of my blood, and pain beyond the reach of morphine. It rooted itself early on in my career and the haunting image of a gory demise was a constant companion. It was a heavy burden to lug around all those years, but it did keep me on my toes and likely saved my life several times along the way. Not an inconsequential thing.

The trip into the Delta has wrapped. To the seasoned journalists, just another day at the *zoo*. As for me, well, I was dragging my ass through the mud and wondering what the hell I'd gotten myself into. There were a lot of places I could be—safe places, nurturing places. Places filled with laughter, joy, love. Still, when I eventually got around to thinking it through, I discovered I was pretty much where I wanted to be, maybe even where I was *meant* to be. Those few hours walking among the dead down in the Delta had me crossing some invisible line, and there was no turning back now.

As the helicopters lift up from the rice paddy and the body of the *child-soldier* fades from view, I'm struck by the absolute beauty of the land streaking by—the distant mountains, the green, broad flat plains crisscrossed by brown canals, and rivulets fed by the Mekong River. Looking down at the lush fields, and those villages which measure time in centuries, there's no evidence of war, only a landscape so tranquil in appearance it makes one forget, if only for a moment or two, the jarring reality unfolding one thousand feet below.

Thirty-Five Years Later… and Half a World Away

Left the interstate at Wytheville and soon people and their clutter are behind me.

Driving along two-lane country roads winding through fertile farmlands and verdant valleys, the hillsides and meadows rich with spring laurel, milkweed and dandelion, the air pure and charged with renewal.

Lose the pavement at the crossroads village of Speedwell and begin moving up the mountain, navigating narrow gravel roads hugging the slopes of deep ravines and meandering hollows, under a leafy canopy of oak, sourwood, blackgum, and spruce, and groves of hemlock, birch and balsam.

The Virginia forest is softly lit this morning, the fragrance of spring powerful in advance of the arrival of the ripeness of full summer. Pastels of spring cascade down the slope into the farm-dotted valleys; migrating black and orange monarch butterflies ride the soft breezes guiding them to their destiny ever farther to the north; a red-shouldered hawk drifts on an updraft, then banks right and streaks earthward, vanishing from view along the tree line; a black bear forages in a bramble patch at the edge of a thicket, seemingly oblivious to the presence of an outsider intruding on its domain, and morning meal. Deer are everywhere.

At the summit, the road disintegrates into little more than a muddy dirt path, tire-rutted and littered with branches from the thunderstorm which swept through the night before.

The leafage quickly closes in tight around me. Extended and overhanging limbs and earth-hugging greenery flick at the car, the undercarriage groaning as it makes contact with the ground rising up to meet it.

The advertising brochure for an "*idyllic top of the world cabin*" sure as hell never mentioned any of this.

I soon pass through the entanglement and emerge back into full sunlight, more than a little disappointed at myself for the unease I felt at a rather harmless encounter with a short stretch of bad road. I tell myself I'd better toughen up, and fast, if this road trip is to have any hope of success.

There was a time I could take on just about any and everything thrown at me, but that was a while ago, involving a different me. It's becoming increasingly apparent I've morphed into a much more cautious, sober guy, and I'm not at all happy about it. I find myself wishing I could be who I once was, but realize I may have no choice but to settle for a watered-down version. The cold reality has sunk in I'm off center stage now, way off, just a nondescript person on a road trip, an old man and damn near invisible on top of everything else.

I'd be the first to concede this journey I cooked up is pretty much a conceptual hodgepodge of disconnected thoughts, romantic notions, and undercooked plans, which common sense dictates is not a prudent approach when stepping off into an unexplored wilderness—even a wilderness where I speak the language, the food is familiar, I can drink the water, read road signs, and where security's not a major issue unless I venture into certain areas of Baltimore.

The trip first began to form in my head as winter surrendered to spring in the North Carolina Sandhills and I found myself in the grip of a restlessness usually reserved for a young person, not someone who'd already put himself out to pasture.

It was pretty clear from the outset I was not a good match with formal retirement. I tried my best to keep the intellectual flame flickering by teaching college for several years, but had grown frustrated by the rigid academic bureaucracy and formalities. Wrote a small-town weekly newspaper column for a year, gave Impressionist oil painting a try, learned to make pewter cutlery, refinish furniture, bake bread...Took on freelance editorial projects, and got in over my head dealing early American antiques, blowing fifty thousand dollars in the process. I attended auctioneering school in New Hampshire for the hell of it. Sold automobiles for two months just to see what it was like on the inside. Not pretty. Made a modest connection with photography and there had been a few gallery shows and some positive reviews. Had several affairs. Still, it was clear something was missing from my life, and I came to realize rather suddenly, and not all that surprisingly, that missing something was, well...me. That was the day the idea of a road trip took its first deep breath.

I guess you could argue the very thought of month after month on the open road was more than a little cockamamie for a man of my years. I was in my sixties now and the passage of time had not ignored me. I was thirty pounds heavier than in my prime. I needed glasses to read. My once full head of hair was thinning, my beard now mostly white. My lungs were frail, the main culprit the two-pack a day cigarette habit I managed to kick *cold turkey* some years earlier. Exposure to teargas and anything else toxic the shitholes of this world could lay on me had also done a number on my ability to suck in sufficient quantities of oxygen. My back had never been the same since a hard helicopter landing in South Korea in the eighties, and there had been several major health scares along the way.

While I may have been an unlikely candidate for a hard year on the open road, the call was alive and throbbing inside me and I was caught up in the moment. When my plan received enthusiastic thumbs up from my three adult children, the final hurdle had been cleared and the road trip was on.

When I got right down to it, there was no question I knew little of my own country. Oh, I was familiar enough with the historical high points, had long since memorized the *Gettysburg Address,* the first few lines to the Preamble to the Constitution, and I could reel off the names of the presidents in order of service. Could probably even name most, if not all, the members of the Supreme Court.

Still, I was pretty much a blank slate in many critical areas. I'd seldom ventured very far west of the Mississippi River, for one. The vast American West was always viewed from thirty thousand feet in a jetliner streaking for some foreign port. I clearly recall thinking then how rugged, barren, harsh, unforgiving, even frightening that land looked so far below. I made a mental note to take the time to explore it one day, then pretty much forget about it for the next few decades. Bigger fish to fry, or so I thought.

In drawing up a broad outline for the road trip, I was determined first and foremost not to be burdened with excessive exactness, to allow spontaneity to point the way. The prime objective would be to move, not arrive some place. Create the initial thrust, then be pulled along in the wake.

When allowing my imagination and romantic nature to rev on high, I envisioned myself unbridled, marching to the beat of my own drum towards distant horizons, the *thump-thump* of road tar strips singing to me, the land sweeping me up in its arms and propelling me forward. I would be guided by unseen forces whispering in my ear. I would travel fast, light, and alone, always heading *towards* a destination than *away* from one. I'd avoid big cities. I'd mostly stick to roads less traveled. Zipping along the Interstate Highway System, that ribbon of soulless concrete for any length of time, would be to turn a blind eye to the potential of what lay close by, off to the sides.

I remembered what the late Charles Kuralt said about this years ago. Thanks to the interstates, he wrote, *"it is now possible to travel across the country from coast to coast without seeing anything."*

I settled on twelve months duration for the road trip for no other reason than it had a nice ring to it. I probably wouldn't be able to see all I wanted to see in a year, but I would squeeze the most out of each day, make every hour and mile count. At least that was the plan.

My three year-old *Mazda3* hatchback would be my transportation. The compact had nearly sixty thousand miles on it by now, but had proven itself to be reliable so I was confident the car could withstand the rigors of the road and keep me mostly safe in the process, provided I didn't bring down a world of hurt on myself.

Susan Heller wrote that when preparing to travel, *"lay out all your clothes and all your money. Then take half the clothes and twice the money."*

Sound advice. All veteran travelers pretty much know that, but it's not always so easy sticking to it.

I instructed myself to be strong, to cart along as little as possible and avoid the temptation to try to cover the multitude of social and environmental situations I knew I'd face out on the road.

I challenged myself to see if I could travel the country on one hundred dollars a day. One hundred for everything, including gasoline. Wouldn't be easy. My life would be a series of fast food restaurants, truck stops, diners, road houses, and scabby motels...but this suited my purpose. I wanted a dramatic lifestyle change, to rub shoulders with things new, not a cocooning in *Holiday Inns* and *Marriott's,* and restaurants with wine lists.

I dismissed the idea of camping on the trip. Only if absolutely necessary, and maybe not even then. I instinctively knew at my age I'd be unable to properly recuperate from a demanding day behind the wheel if I were deprived of a hot shower to wash away the road film and a non-rocky landscape on which to lay my head.

I settled on late-May as the time to hit the road. Around Memorial Day. That was a month off, and there was plenty to do before then.

Had my car checked out by the local dealership, and bought new tires. A powerful flashlight was a must, along with several cans of *Fix-a-Flat,* road flares, snake bite kit, hunting knife, compass, altimeter, walking stick, and binoculars. I packed a blanket, along with a pillow and pair of sheets for those times when motel linens offended, and shelled out for a sleeping bag in the event I ever found myself under attack by bed bugs and had to seek refuge on the floor, or in the car.

I shopped for rugged hiking boots, purchased a small selection of practical everyday sports shirts, jeans and no-iron khaki slacks. I added a windbreaker and light jacket to get me started. I could always buy anything else I needed out on the road, where I was sure I'd be encountering a Walmart every five or ten miles.

Scratched off the clothing list were suits, blazers, ties, dress slacks, tasseled loafers, and any piece of clothing which included the words *cashmere, silk, linen, or polyester.*

I picked up a six hundred dollar *Pentax* SLR digital camera, and replaced my old cell phone for one with GPS. For a five dollar monthly fee, I added a locator service to the phone which would allow family members to track down my remains should I slip and fall unnoticed into the Grand Canyon.

I also purchased a tiny digital voice recorder for when I wanted to dictate notes, or surreptitiously capture conversations with people I'd meet out on the road. Once a journalist, always a journalist.

The road trip now needed something to hang its hat on. A personality. A job, if you will. Nothing too complicated, or daring. Just enough of a challenge to keep me alert and involved as the miles ticked off; a project which would permit the creative juices to flow in modest measure, and help make me feel less like a rootless bum as the months roll by. I decide to focus on *photographing* the landscapes, small towns, and people I'd encounter along the way, subjects which would always be at my fingertips, from beginning to end.

Let me add here I certainly didn't dismiss the enormity of the road trip, all that it would entail, and the demands it would place on me. It would be hard work. That was clear. I fully anticipated there'd be moments which would sap my strength and commitment, and I'd toy with the idea of ending my travels right then and there. I'd fight it, of course, but there's really no way of knowing how such battles would ultimately play out. To a younger me, hardships amounted to little more than a slight annoyance. To the older me, well, that had yet to be determined.

Bottom line. It was time now to discover what I had left in the tank. I prayed it was more than just fumes.

My car's coated in a thin layer of rust-colored dust by the

time I reach the small rental cabin, perched on a knoll in the middle of a large clearing, atop a mountain nestled in the midst of still other blue-tinged peaks.

The cabin's rustic-perfect. The nearest neighbor's eight miles away.

I quickly unpack the car and collapse on the first bunk bed I come to. Emotional fatigue more than anything else. I was drained. One of the first serious indications I had that age would be a factor in my travels and that I should probably start making allowances for it when mapping out each new day.

I'm hardly thrilled at yet another confirmation I'm no longer young. I just hope I'll be able to rein in my natural instinct to push myself to the limit. I'm fully aware a steady, measured pace will produce better results over the long haul than racing about willy-nilly without regard for my limitations...but I also know I don't always listen to myself, especially if it involves accepting a downsizing.

I awaken to a hard rain which quickly fades to a drizzle, then exits off to the northeast. The mountain air took on a chill during my nap so I toss some logs into the great stone fireplace and soon have a fire going to be proud of.

The atmosphere's still unsettled and restless as day surrenders to night. I'm sitting on the porch steps, wrapped in a blanket, sipping a beer straight from the bottle, watching the distant mountains quiver in the fading light, as an earth-hugging fog bank crawls up the western slope of the mountain and rolls in over my feet.

-II-

"There are three rules to writing...
Unfortunately, no one knows what they are."
~W. Somerset Maugham

This Morning

It's four-thirty. I've been at it for the past six hours. I'm writing at this ungodly hour because I've come to realize the so-called "creative process" cannot be expected to follow a timetable. It happens when it happens, and I have no real choice but to respond to the call regardless of the hour if I ever want to actually finish this book.

Of course, there's no sure-fire way to tell if what I'm working on will hold up to critical scrutiny by the time the day ends. A writer's only as good as his words, of course, but since the offspring of this process is pretty much subjective anyway, the only strategy which makes any sense at all to me is to just do it and hope for the best.

A major hurdle I face in writing an actual book, even a short one such as this, is I'm traveling down a new path and my instincts in this area are nowhere as well-honed as I would like. A broadcast journalist, I spent my *entire* career dispensing information in as few words as possible. Strong emphasis on the word *few*. Given the limitations of time in broadcast news, a compact gathering of words is crucial. Writing an actual book with an abundance of words in complex combinations is a whole new ballgame and requires a major retooling of the skill set, and a heartless shedding of old habits...although I'm starting to conclude many of those old ways just may plan on hanging around regardless of what I may want.

Maybe it would be a good idea at this stage of the process to just kick back a little and reel off some short bursts of filtered insights into my character, habits, attitudes, where I stand on various issues, along with whatever else may pop into my head. If you're going to spend your valuable time reading this little book, it seems only fair to let you know where I'm coming from, where I stand, and maybe heading, although your enlightenment is hardly a given...

- First, I'd like to make it perfectly clear that half of what's been said about me over the years is simply untrue. Unfortunately, the other half *is* true.
- I'm biodegradable.
- I dislike losing more than I like winning.
- Conservative friends are convinced I'm a Liberal. Liberal friends are convinced I'm a Conservative.
- Can't say I'm affiliated with any political party. I like some of what every party says it'll do for us if elected. Problem is I like even *less* of what they promise.
- The world would be in far better shape if women were the sole gender allowed to hold public office.
- The state of journalism is appalling, and deeply troubling.
- I'm convinced even modest viewing of MSNBC and Fox News can trigger testicular shrinkage.

- I miss Walter Cronkite.
- I no longer mow lawns, shovel snow, lift furniture, jog, go bare-chested in public, or make-out in the backseat of cars.
- I'm comfortable in my own skin. I just wish there were less of it.
- I believe in reincarnation. I live with shadows from a rural life centuries ago.
- I do not regret one enemy. They made me stronger.
- I never obeyed all the rules. So much of life would have been missed if I had.
- I've been married twice, divorced twice. I like to think no one was at fault, but deep down I know better.
- I can look at my children and tell they're mine.
- I do not object at all to women calling the shots in bed. They know far better than I do what they like, and how to get there, so I'm perfectly content at this stage of the game to simply be the vessel on which they sail.
- It should come as no surprise I have far more female friends than male ones.
- My second wife was an actual countess from the Principality of Monaco. I hoped the marriage would make me a count, but Prince Rainier didn't think that was such a good idea.
- I once had a pet monkey named *Suzy Wong*.
- Attended the same high school as Warren Buffett.
- Ava Gardner's sister delivered my baby diapers.
- One of Susan Sarandon's sisters cuts my hair.
- I've never met Sharon Stone, but I've seen all her movies.
- My sister and Bo Derek are good friends, but my sister never alerts me when Bo's a house guest. I guess she knows me all too well.

- At a Nazi memorabilia auction some time back, I was high bidder on a pair of Eva Braun's monogrammed lace panties. Sold the historic undergarment when my girlfriend showed no interest in wearing it.
- I like that being old permits me to get away with pretty much anything.
- I find the older I get, the easier it is to laugh at myself.
- I've lived longer than I thought I would.
- Many friends have described me as an *Old Soul.* That's okay, I guess, but I'm not thrilled when called an *Old Fool* or *Old Fart.* Perfectly acceptable and even welcomed, however, is *Old Fuck.*
- For some reason, I'm unable to keep my right shoelace tied for any extended period of time.
- The *good side* of my face was once the left side, but that was before skin cancer consumed my left ear and no plastic surgeon could put it back the way it was. That left me with no *good side.*
- Nature is far more generous to us than we are to her. On *Arbor Day,* I make a point to pause for a moment to *thank* Mother Nature. On *Earth Day,* I make a point to pause for a moment to *apologize* to Mother Nature.
- I've never been to Cincinnati.
- I don't care what anyone says...I still consider Pluto a planet.
- Eat grits nearly every single day.
- I consume way too much goat cheese.
- I've been arrested twice, but never served any jail time.
- I have an uncanny gift of being able to stop a fast-flowing gas pump on an even dollar amount.
- I can count to ten in Farsi.
- At one time I stood six-foot-three.

- Baseball's my game. Worshipped Mickey Mantle as a kid, and still do. Ted Williams was the greatest hitter ever. The thought of his severed head bobbing around in a vat of liquid nitrogen at a cryonics company is horrifying.
- One birthday, a girlfriend paid good money to have my name attached to a star in the Milky Way Galaxy. Given the rocky state of our relationship at the time, I suspect she held out hope I'd actually move there.
- A few of my contemporaries: Diane Sawyer, George Lucas, Jerry Springer, Michael Douglas, Angela Davis, Sirhan Sirhan, James Carville, Lou Dobbs, Van Morrison, Sally Field, Steve Martin, Sylvester Stallone, Richard Leaky, Helen Mirren, Joe Pesci, Tom Selleck, Doris Kearns Goodwin, Goldie Hawn, Liza Minnelli, Rod Stewart, William Calley, Oliver North, Carly Simon, Bette Midler, Sam Shepard, Barry Manilow, Woodward and Bernstein...
- I'm related to Presidents James Madison, Andrew Johnson, and Zachary Taylor, along with Jefferson Davis...Madison, *The Father of the Constitution,* died flat broke; Lincoln's successor was impeached by the House of Representatives; *Old Rough and Ready* died just a few months into his presidency after guzzling too much ice water on a hot summer day; and the face of the Confederate States of America was arrested while trying to flee the country dressed as a woman. Always something.
- I was fired as a *Good Humor Man* when I was eighteen for eating all the profits by the time I returned the ice cream truck to the lot each evening.
- I accidentally burned Fabian's hand with a cigarette in nineteen sixty-one.

- I had a high school crush on Connie Stevens. Met her at a cocktail party in Tokyo a quarter century later and told her about it. She wasn't impressed.
- Favorite Movie (tie): *The Best Years of Our Lives, Mrs. Miniver, Key Largo, The Quiet Man,* and *The Searchers.*
- Favorite Movie Line: *"I'd like to kiss you, but I just washed my hair."*
- Mononucleosis forced me to miss my high school prom.
- Recognize a dewberry when I see one.
- A flight attendant once told me I look like Anthony Hopkins.
- I panic when my face makes contact with a spider web.
- *If* I played golf, I'd play left-handed.
- Told I speak French like a Spanish cow.
- As of this writing, I have one hundred sixty-six Facebook "friends." I even know a few of them.
- Abraham Lincoln, Robert E. Lee, Winston Churchill, Mahatma Gandhi, Thomas Jefferson, George Washington, John Adams, Benjamin Franklin, Leonardo da Vinci, Emile Zola, Eleanor Roosevelt, and Paul Robeson are *among* the historical figures I most admire.
- I've lived in, or set foot in, more than eighty countries, principalities, and territories, chalking up unimaginable air miles in the process.
- My passport expired years ago. Discarded it after a miserable seventeen-hour flight from Johannesburg to Miami, and I haven't flown since. If I'm unable to reach a destination these days by automobile, train, bus, boat, bike, foot, skateboard, pogo stick, horseback, or dog-sled, I simply don't go.
- I was conceived October sixteenth, nineteen forty-three, at the *St. George Hotel* in Brooklyn Heights, New York.

I know this because my mother told me so. No sane person wants to know the first thing about their parents' sex life, but she told me anyway, even after I crawled into a fetal position and begged mercy. Anyway, turns out the *St. George* was quite the grand palace back in forty-three. The largest hotel in the country. Thirty stories high. High society danced in the ballroom. Presidents overnighted there. Famous writers and artists, too. Fitzgerald, Hemingway. Truman Capote swam in the art deco pool. Leonard Bernstein conducted the New York Philharmonic on site. Scenes from *The Godfather* were filmed at the hotel...The world was deep at war that October day so long ago and the ultimate outcome of the conflagration still far from certain. My parents had spent only a few weeks together since they married two days before the attack on Pearl Harbor, so any time cobbled together was precious. My dad was on shore leave that week I came into being. He was a naval gunnery officer on the *USS Winfield Scott,* which escorted cargo ships through the treacherous North Atlantic, where U-Boats roamed. My mom was a secretary at the Newport News Shipyards. Three days post-conception, my dad was back out at sea, and my mom and I were on a packed train heading for Virginia, she on a hard seat, me safe and warm in her womb. I've pretty much been on the move ever since.

-III-

The Road Trip Journal

Entry 1: First full day on the Virginia mountaintop. Beautiful morning. Sunny. Nice breeze. Air rich with spring flavors. Slept like a baby. Invigorated and eager to begin my *new* life.

This is the start of a *Journal* of the road trip. The very first entry. Idea came to me overnight. Lots of miles lay ahead and I'd like to keep at least some record of the trip beyond photographs.

The only concern I have is the time it takes to write will detract from the journey I really want to take, which is one of being overwhelmed visually. Right now, images come first, words second, although that could change by the time all is said and done. Hopefully, there's a happy medium. Images by day, words by night? That may work.

Thinking along the lines of jotting down my experiences, thoughts and observations from time to time in my laptop when the mood strikes. It certainly won't be an everyday thing...and it won't be silkily-written, that's for sure...not at the end of a long, hard day on the road when fatigue is washing over me, but I'll do the best I can, and my apologies in advance to any high school English teachers out there who may one day get their hands on a copy of this journal. They're forewarned they run the risk of stroking out by what's heading their way. Grammar and spelling are not exactly long suits, tense deployment can be unpredictable and conflicting, and my punctuation is all over the map. I use an inordinate number of dots and dashes and odd sentence structures, a habit picked up writing broadcast news. Tells me when to break, place emphasis, and breathe when reading copy on the air. To add to the muddle, I've never advocated requiring each and every sentence contain actual nouns and verbs, to number in excess of one word, or less than two hundred, and I don't consider adjectives strung together in copious numbers to be a literary felony.

If that weren't enough, I've been known to invent words out of the blue. "*Yulinate,*" for example, is one such concoction. In my universe, it means to sing Christmas carols in the bathroom. Word just popped into my head one Christmas Eve years ago in Bangkok while standing at the *can* humming "*chestnuts roasting on an open fire...*" So, should a reader happen across a word they're unable to locate in *Webster's*, they can be confident of its origin, and take comfort that its unfamiliarity does not constitute a hole in the wealth of their vocabulary.

Oh, one final admonition. While I'll do my best to keep the journal light, informal and breezy, I reserve the right to texture it up when unable to resist the temptation to uncork one.

That said, let's roll...

Well, here I am! Must say the cabin's not at all bad. Unadorned, maybe, but not uncivilized. Just enough of a compromise to convince myself I'm "roughing it," but not so much I feel as if I've been totally abandoned by the past two centuries.

No potable water means I can forget about taking showers. Mercifully, there's a water system of some kind which allows me to flush the toilet, and the cabin has electricity. That permits, among other things, lights, refrigerator, and microwave. No Daniel Boone experience awaits me here.

Had been alerted in advance about the drinking water situation so carted in twenty or so gallon plastic jugs. First thing this morning heated a pot of water on the stove, took it outside where I stripped all the way down and gave myself a sponge bath. Felt uncomfortable hanging out like that in the open air. No telling what eyes were on me from the surrounding woods, or satellites above. Think I'll just take my sponge bath tomorrow standing in the never used bathtub, provided I can work up the enthusiasm to remove all the insects which went there to die.

Tried my cell phone. No signal. No landline phone. No internet and no television either, but there's a radio, a small table model by the window in the living room. Pretty much the only station I can pick up with any authority is a *country* one in some distant valley. Must say the music makes for pretty good company, even if it's honkytonk.

Can't get over the solitude up here. I feel as if I'm in the very bowels of nature. An astonishing place to find myself. Noticed right away the mountains and valleys, woods and fields, ponds and streams, all somehow look and act differently up here. Far more confident and at ease than they are in the world I just left behind, where they mostly serve as backdrops and garnishes, not the center attraction.

Difficult to believe it was just yesterday when I launched this trip. Seems more like, well, I'm not sure, but certainly more than a single day.

Maybe it would be a good idea now to play catch-up with that first day on the road for the sake of this journal. I don't want day one clouded by time and failing memory years from now, so need to get it down right away...

Yesterday. The approaching dawn is little more than a faint

pink ribbon hugging the bottom rung of the horizon when I hit the road.

I manage to slip out of town without fanfare. Just me, alone. No bands, no media, no family or friends seeing me off at that early hour.

I move fast through the Sandhills, driving northwest, dew-covered peach orchards and vineyards off to the sides.

Feels good finally having the road under me, the *Mazda* yielding to every command. An exhilarating sense of freedom and anticipation. I'm thirsting for all the tomorrows to come.

Then, there's the ever-present question bouncing around in my head, one I can't quite seem to shake:

"So, what the hell am I doing?!"

Let's review this one final time just for the record. *Old guy uproots himself and heads down the road with only the vaguest notion where he's going, what he plans to do when he gets there, or what he'll do when all is said and done.*

I guess that pretty much covers it.

If I had any sense at all, I should be shitting enough bricks along about now to build the Great Wall of China, not that any of the obvious shortcomings in my planning will deter me. I'm totally committed to this journey. Besides, it's too late to turn back now.

Forced to park on the side of the road during a vicious cloudburst in Winston-Salem, spot Pilot Mountain when the dull, dark skies begin to clear, and reach Fancy Gap an hour after sunrise. Pull over when I spot an old woman hauling glass jugs of apple cider from a pickup truck to an open-sided fruit and vegetable stand.

"We ain't open yet!" Her voice is authoritative, booming. I'd bet she'd raised half a dozen kids and taken no shit from any of them.

“Yes, I know, but I’m heading into the mountains for a few weeks and would appreciate it if...”

“Okay,” she says, exasperated, “but you gotta have the exact amount. My husband’s waiting for the bank to open later to bring me some small bills for change.”

“Yes, that’ll be fine. Thanks.”

She hands me a few brown paper bags. “You do your own pickin’ here. Don’t want no one complaining later if a bruised piece of fruit turns up.”

I examine the plastic bins and reed baskets stacked high with assorted varieties of tomatoes, bell peppers, potatoes, yams, onions, berries, squash...Then there’s the honey and molasses, assorted relishes, and pretty much anything else coming out of a farmhouse kitchen which can be stuffed into a *Mason Jar*. I ask if everything is grown locally.

“Farmers around these parts come in two, three times a week with stuff they growed,” she answers. “Some of it in the fields, some in greenhouses. I even growed some of the vegetables myself. Usually stick to squash. They’re pretty easy. Sorry to say I don’t do near as much as I used to. Gettin’ old, I guess, but I still like digging into the dirt with my hands when my arthritis ain’t acting up bad on me, and the weather’s nice. No siree, you’ll find nothing sold on this mountain needing a passport to get into the country. Enough of that nonsense going on already.”

I select five fat tomatoes the color of a glowing fire, drop a jar of clover honey and two scoops of baby potatoes into a bag, and cradle a seedless watermelon in my arms.

I examine the jars of pickled boiled eggs floating in beet juice which has transformed the egg whites into a soothing pink fuchsia.

“Three each for the eggs, or two for five-fifty,” she informs me. “Half dozen eggs or thereabouts in each. They can last a long time bottled like that. Don’t even need no refrigeration.”

“You sure they’re safe?”

“Oh, yes. Been eatin’ them that way all my life. Never made me sick, not even once. Friend of mine did those particular ones. Millie and me went to school together and she married my cousin Earl. He died of a stroke the day after Thanksgiving last, so the eggs bring in a little extra money for her. She sure can use it. Hard times since Earl passed on so Millie may have to take in boarders.”

I take two jars of the pickled eggs, calculating they’d be good travel companions. The Millie story also played a role.

“You’ll like ‘em,” she promises. “The bitter taste may take some gettin’ used to, but you can rinse them off with water if you have a mind to. Sure you don’t want another jar or two? You don’t want to run out of easy stuff to eat wherever it is you’re heading.”

“Sure, why not.”

The old woman is busy stacking vegetables in tall mounds I’m convinced gravity will conspire to topple, but they prove as durable as the pyramids.

“So, where you from?” she asks.

I sense she’s actually beginning to warm up to me, but that could be an illusion created by the early hour and thin mountain air.

“Oh, no place in particular,” I answer. “Moved around a lot during my life. Big cities mostly, but I’ve been down in Southern Pines the past few years.”

“I just can’t understand why people want to live in big cities like they do. No siree, here’s plenty fine and more than enough for me. I was born right here, growed up here, raised a family here, and I’m gonna die and be buried right here.”

The bill comes to twenty-four dollars. I hand her a twenty and a ten, which she quickly pockets.

"You have a safe trip now, you hear."

Connect with the Blue Ridge Parkway and drive along the crest of a stretch of the six hundred mile long, unbroken two-lane road weaving through the heavily-forested mountain range.

Find sections around campgrounds and rest areas too civilized and theatrically-staged for my taste, but the road grows more interesting the deeper I drive into the old growth forest. Less evidence of us. A more measured and natural rhythm of life.

The forest is busy birthing and rearing a new generation. White-tailed fawn fearlessly bound down the middle of the Parkway kicking their hoofs high in youthful exuberance, with agitated mothers in hot pursuit, all of which makes driving a white-knuckle experience. Can't begin to count the number of chipmunks and squirrels darting across the road, snakes out sunning on the warm pavement, and curious groundhogs, rabbits, skunks, possums and raccoons eyeballing me as I breeze by.

Since views of distant mountains ranges, and the valleys below, are shielded by the increasingly dense foliage, making photography difficult and generally uninteresting, I promise myself to return some autumn for the unveiling of the broad brush strokes of red, orange, and yellow. Should be quite a show.

It's not even noon when I left the Parkway and set out to explore some back roads. Lots of farms and barns and one-horse towns. Don't remember much about it. Too excited. Mind racing ahead, unable to settle into the new reality.

Check into a cheap motel towards nightfall. End up at one of those tired, old backwater places bypassed by the Interstate Highway System, along with the second half of the twentieth-century.

Think Hitchcock's *Bates Motel*, then think *really* creepy. I would have barricaded the bathroom door when I took a shower had there been a bathroom door.

The bad-tempered geezer running the place, a fellow with fewer teeth than a cat has lives, looks at me like I'm a Martian when I ask if they have wireless internet.

Pillows are like bricks, sheets threadbare, the mattress sags, the bedspring squeaks, but I don't much care. Sleep comes easy.

Entry 2: Third morning on the mountain. Roll over in bed and through the window see threads of white streaking across the face of a pink moon suspended low over the mountain range out to the east. It's nearly four. Throw on a robe and race outside. Stand barefoot in the cold, dew-covered grass and am treated a spectacular meteor shower. Can't get back to sleep so wait up for the sunrise. It doesn't disappoint. I sure could get used to this.

Entry 3: I'm starting to pay attention to the clouds. Restless and boisterous one minute, content to loiter the next. Great subjects for photography, particularly as they saunter by in the early morning, and deep into the evening, when the evolving natural light strokes them in unexpected ways.

Must watch water consumption. Really don't need those daily sponge baths. Who's around anyway to care if I stink? I certainly don't.

Food's holding up okay. Managing to eat healthy. Dropping pounds. Body feels better for it. I do miss ice cream, however.

Radio's my sole contact with the outside world, but make a point to turn it off when the music stops and news begins. Knowing what's going on down below is not a high priority right now. Quite a dramatic change in habit and attitude for the first week. Didn't see that one coming, but hope it lasts.

I'm actually growing quite fond of country music. I'm especially drawn to the unpretentious, universal lyrics. My life story, everyone's life story, put to music.

Sleeping a good eight hours a night. Haven't done that in years. Bladder's even cooperating.

With all this quiet time available to meditate and reflect, it's really starting to sink in what I've taken on. I just hope my resolve is equal to my determination. One positive early sign: I'm not second-guessing my decision to stretch myself. That bodes well for the future. In fact, I'm increasingly confident I have it in me to complete the mission, provided nothing jumps out of the bushes to bite me in the ass.

And with that I'll say goodnight.

Entry 4: The first rays of light playing off distant mountains is a wonderful way to start a day. The human hand has barely touched this patch of earth. Not many places remain like this, as far as I know, and that's a real shame. We're certainly not good caretakers of all the bounty and I suspect nature will someday have its fill of us and brush us aside like an annoying gnat.

Have to watch where I step right now. Monarch butterflies are everywhere. Great clouds of them. They like to congregate in groups on the ground and dance around one another, almost playfully. I suspect there's some heavy-duty communicating going on. Just wish I were privy.

Lots of bats here. Silent, ghostly shadows zipping about in

the gloaming. Never did much like them for obvious reasons, but starting to better appreciate how the bat fits into the grand scheme of things, and how we all benefit. Proof of that is I'm not buried right now under a blizzard of blood-sucking insects.

Entry 5: Days now without seeing another living soul. But for the twinkling lights in the valleys below, it would be easy to think I'm all alone on this planet.

The nights on this peak are as mysterious as distant worlds, the darkness inexplicable to someone accustomed to life in the populated, twitchy bottomlands, where night is really never night in the true sense of the word. We disturb the natural balance by slicing into the darkness with manufactured light, seldom appreciating or marveling that the unadulterated night is as full of promise, and as richly-colored, as any bright day could ever hope to be.

Then there are the *sounds* of nature. The pulse around me is measured, distinct, sturdy, and close. Sometimes too close. No end of cries, hisses, grunts, howls, and rustling in the fields and forests at night. Tempted to investigate, but that may not be such a good idea. Not sure what I'd find or, worse, what would find me.

Lazy days spent exploring the surrounding woods or sitting on the porch reading *Men Against the Sea* for maybe the tenth time since I first picked up the book when I was a boy. Men adrift in a small boat in the far reaches of the vast South Pacific, battling impossible odds but persevering and ultimately conquering the elements, and their demons.

Thought I spotted a bobcat pass over a rocky outcropping around sundown. A fleeting glimpse. These wild animals are not very social. Can't say I blame them. We humans are not exactly in lockstep harmony with nature around us and these creatures sense that and give us wide berth.

Have come to realize that while nature certainly isn't benevolent, it's never shallow or vindictive. Understand that, give nature the proper respect and deference up here in the clouds, and you should make out just fine.

I had erroneously assumed the fortress-like doors to the cabin were there to discourage visits from the cast of *Deliverance*, not fend off marauding bears anxious to climb into bed with me in the middle of the night. A notice tacked to the bulletin board in the utility room set me straight on that. Double-checking the doors now before I hit the sack, just in case.

Seen three bears so far, and suspect far *more* of them have seen me. Thankfully, they've kept their distance. Hope it stays that way. Making sure I store away the food at night just in case. Leaving nothing lying around. Sure way to ask for trouble. When they've locked onto the scent of something to eat, bears come at you like a runaway train.

Weather's been just perfect during my time here. Warm days, "sweater weather" evenings, and chilly nights curled up under a mountain of blankets. The amount of stress and angst I've been able to shed amazes me. I never realized I was carting around so heavy a load.

My little cabin has become quite special to me, but the time has come to move on...

Entry 6: In a motel on the rice plains of Arkansas, just west of Memphis. I left the cabin well before dawn today and headed southwest through the Great Appalachian Valley, breezing through a light fog blanketing the rich farmlands, once a major source of food for the Confederacy.

Didn't pause for the Great Smokey's and Tennessee, promising to return later when the thick greenery of late-spring no longer hides the land from my eyes.

Stopped for an early dinner at *Loretta Lynn's Kitchen* in Hurricane Mills. Yep, that's country signer Loretta Lynn, the coal miner's daughter. She's from around these parts and her ranch is just up the road a piece.

Food at her restaurant's pure *downhome*. Ordered a country fried steak, okra, sugar snap peas, hot biscuits lathered in fresh butter and smothered in white gravy. Finished up with chocolate cream pie. Could actually hear my arteries snapping shut.

Met my goal to cross the Mississippi River by dusk. My little *Mazda* ate up the miles without protest.

Increasingly anxious now to shift this road trip into a higher gear.

Entry 7: Three days now since I left the mountain. Entering country I've never seen before. Flat, barren and, quite frankly, boring. I confess to being underwhelmed so far by Oklahoma.

The fault's mine, actually, for failing to do my homework, resulting in vastly over-inflated expectations. Oklahoma's serving up in small doses what I'd anticipated in dramatic, high relief—mountain ranges, canyons, and boisterous rivers. Instead, all I'm running across are geographically dispersed low-end bits and pieces, but hopefully an *amuse bouche* to the eye-popping grandeur I hope awaits me down the road. If I'm wrong about that, then I'm in for a very long year.

Where Oklahoma shines, however, is the expanse of sky. It

goes on forever, accented with puffy clouds propelled along by determined winds whistling across the ranch lands.

Can't help but think of the Great Depression and the Dust Bowl years, and those poor people tragically beaten down by the economy and weather. It was right here, in the very spot, the Depression hit hardest. The drought-triggered massive dust storms of the nineteen thirties blew away precious top soil from overused lands and quickly turned the Great Plains into a desert which, combined with the deepening national economic crisis, broke the backs of untold numbers of already desperately poor tenant farmers, forcing them off the land, and triggering the historic migration to California.

The vast plains, prairies, and fields are lush now, the physical and emotional scars healed, at least to my untrained eye.

Overnighting in a place called Henryetta, Troy Aikman's boyhood home. Toyed with the idea of dropping by the Aikman homestead, but the thought quickly passed. Maybe next time.

Entry 8: Approaching the Texas Panhandle the wind's making itself known. Before I realize it, a full-blown dust storm's on the rampage. Dry lightning's sparking wildfires and hurricane force winds urge on the infernos. Towns are threatened. Homes have burned. Several people have died. Giant wads of tumbleweed bounce down the highway. High profile trucks have flipped on their sides. The sun's swallowed by a deep-red, swirling cloud stretching from horizon to horizon.

Pull over at a highway rest stop to wait out the weather. Sprinting to the bathroom, a fierce gust of wind slams me into an adobe wall, chipping a tooth and cutting my tongue. My mouth fills with blood and sand. My sunglasses are swept away into the maelstrom.

Entry 9: Heard on the radio this morning that Nelson Mandela is ill. A respiratory ailment of some kind. Didn't catch if he were hospitalized.

Difficult to imagine a South Africa without Mandela. He's the mortar which holds that fragile society together. His departure would trigger God only knows what. He's in his nineties now so I suspect it won't be all that long before the questioned is answered.

I was considered a veteran correspondent by the time I reached South Africa in the summer of nineteen-ninety. Four years in Tokyo reporting bone dry economic news and a few more back in Washington working in an editorial and management capacity had been a colossal bore, but I was now back in my element. I was missing the action. I just hope I retained enough foot speed and mental agility to stay out of real trouble.

It's a time of dramatic transition in South Africa, from a suffocating white-ruled government to a so-called multi-racial democracy, but not everyone's on board with the plan, not by a long shot. It will be a long, difficult road, and many will die.

Most people, at least those with an ounce of common sense and moral fiber, pray Mandela's recent release from twenty-seven years behind prison bars will be the catalyst enabling the country to navigate the final mile to racial sanity.

When I first arrived on the scene, Mandela's African National Congress, now legalized by the white government, was busy setting up shop out of a downtown high-rise office building in Johannesburg. No longer forced to conduct guerrilla operations from neighboring countries and the black townships surrounding all the big South African cities, the A.N.C. is now free to tweak the government's nose in full public view and mostly get away with it.

In a stroke of bad luck, I was felled by double pneumonia when I reached Johannesburg and spent the next three weeks in bed before I could even consider getting down to work. By the time I was back on my wobbly legs, there was a lot of catching up to do. To accomplish that, I'm forced into quick study mode. This means it's imperative to show my face all around town, interview every news-maker I can corner, pour over the newspapers, scan every press release crossing my desk, pick the brains of members of the foreign and local press, all of whom know a hell of a lot more than I do and probably always will, plus attend every press conference possible, even those of marginal interest. Every scrap of information gleaned from the parties to the upcoming talks aimed at eradicating decades of apartheid is crucial to doing my job.

One day very early on in my recovery, I'm sitting in the waiting room of the African National Congress headquarters, doing a slow burn. The press conference had been scheduled for noon and it's now well past one. Normally, I wouldn't put up with such crap, but I need to make up for all that lost time so there I sit, thumbing through a magazine, still feeling weak from the lingering effects of the pneumonia.

A few journalists huddle in a far corner of the room, speaking in quiet tones, but most of the others have long since drifted away. My irritation grows by the minute, fueled by a rare splitting headache.

Then a voice.

"What's going on?"

It's a soft voice, somewhat high-pitched. I don't bother looking up from the magazine. I assume it's another journalist checking back in.

"Still waiting for the presser. Big surprise there, huh? I tell you if the A.N.C. can't get its *fucking* act together, how can it ever expect to run this *fucking* country?!"

"Yes, I better go see what the delay is," comes the reply.

I look up and into the face of Nelson Mandela. He's smiling, a twinkle in his eye, clearly enjoying the look of horror on my face.

And as quick as that he's gone, moving down the long corridor in his trademark stiff, short strides, leaving me sitting there wishing for death.

Postscript:

Two years later, as the country edges ever closer to a non-racial democracy and the white-led government is about to be shown the door by Mandela's movement, I'm summoned to the Mandela home in Soweto Township early one Sunday morning.

I have no clue what it's about. I'm just hoping for an opportunity to quiz Mandela on an upcoming by-election, a crucial step leading to national elections down the road. Maybe if I hit the jackpot, I can get a one-on-one with the man himself, but that may be asking too much. That's the *Holy Grail* for all journalists. While I'd been extensively covering Mandela from one end of South Africa to another, I never managed to land an exclusive interview. Maybe today would be the day.

I always felt uneasy driving in Soweto, or any of the other black townships. The potential for trouble always exists, but it's normally pretty quiet this early on a Sunday, which is the time the unsettled townships across South Africa devote to mopping up the blood shed the night before.

Mandela lives in a gated home in a neighborhood of Soweto known as *Beverly Hills*. It's the best available for well-to-do blacks, but falls short of the lifestyle many whites enjoy just a few miles away.

Even my Spanish-style home in affluent suburban Sandton is substantially larger, and comes equipped with a swimming pool, three-room cabana, lighted tennis court, servants' quarters, and nearly two acres of land for my three watch dogs to roam. Of course, I live behind a high wall and a series of "rape gates," iron doors strategically placed around the house designed to ensure a happy ending to a night of sleep in the crime-riddled country.

I enter the foyer and hear Mandela call down from the top of the stairs. "Is he here?"

I can only see his legs. He's dressed in pajamas. Red and white striped ones, I seem to recall. But it's Mandela. No disguising that voice.

"Yes, Madiba," answers a young aide.

"I'll be down soon. Please offer him some coffee or tea."

I'm ushered into the dining room and asked to sit. I'm there alone. No competition. I can't believe my good luck. I hope it holds.

A few minutes later a beaming Mandela appears, dressed in a beige silk shirt and tan slacks. I stand to attention.

He enthusiastically shakes my hand. "Well, hello, hello, hello! Thank you for coming on such short notice."

"My pleasure, sir."

He motions me to sit and then takes the chair beside mine, pulls it close and leans forward, his face no more than a foot away. "My friend, I have been meaning to ask you something for a long time now," he says in a near whisper.

"Yes, sir."

Mandela's smile is a broad one. "I have not forgotten our *first* meeting. It was most memorable. I have thought of it often."

My groan is audible.

Mandela lays a hand on my shoulder. "So, my friend, tell me how do *you* think *we're* doing *now*?"

Entry 10: Starting to pick up surviving stretches of *Route 66*. Some portions run under a mile, while others eat up huge chunks of neglected asphalt in back-country areas.

The *Mother Road* began as an engine of westward expansion, later a lifeline for those several hundred thousand displaced farmers fleeing to California during the Great Depression, and then it went on to pay host to a cocky nation on the move and flexing its new-found muscles as an emerging economic and military superpower.

Not many kicks to be had these days on *Route 66*, however. The coming of the Interstate Highway System starting back in the nineteen-fifties ultimately spelled doom for the legendary road which once stretched from Chicago to Santa Monica. Aside from small, select sections now undergoing restoration and renovation to try to tempt the nostalgic tourist trade, the remainder is mostly renamed country roads littered with collapsed, shuttered and decaying stores, boarded-up gas stations and rotting tourist courts, intersecting struggling small towns which once prospered catering to the lucrative traffic flow, but are now mostly forgotten remnants of a discarded past. It's a sorry scene.

I can't resist checking out *66* whenever I come across a surviving stretch. Very challenging trying to follow the route now. There are times *66* runs parallel to the interstate, just feet away, but it can drift off on its own, cutting through untamed country, briefly reasserting its dominance, until it's again absorbed by the interstate, or abruptly comes to an unannounced dead end out in the middle of nowhere. Find I'm doing a lot of back-tracking, but I don't mind. It's fun, actually.

It's not an easy mental proposition leaving behind the security of the interstate for the unknown, but the traveler willing to accept the challenge is usually rewarded. When rolling down largely forgotten stretches of *66*, it's impossible not to imagine one's self on this very road decades ago, driving through deserts, hypnotic grasslands and plains, moving along in the shadow of great looming buttes and tablelands, through sunbaked canyons and gorges, over creek beds and dry washes, great distances between gas stations, and no way to summon help in an emergency.

While it was a challenging enough journey for the everyday traveler, it was far worse in the nineteen-thirties for the destitute, uprooted farmers from Oklahoma and Arkansas, at the mercy of the elements, rattletrap cars and ancient trucks, and hostile communities along the route. But onward they came, a wave of humanity reaching out for a new life, but unsure if they'll make it, and what awaits them if they do.

Entry 11: Rolling down the west-bound highway through the Texas Panhandle, making pretty good time in spite of intermittent showers and heavy truck traffic, when I decide to take a break—maybe get a cold drink, something to eat, and then put in some casual back road miles on a long section of *66* which runs somewhat parallel to *I-40* along this stretch of pavement.

Pull off at the first exit I come to and find myself in the town of McLean.

Approaching the business district, I spot three men in a backyard with long knives fucking up the butchering of a huge, screeching, blood-soaked white hog. I look the other way and speed up. Words fail me here.

McLean visually reminds me of the fictitious town in *The Last Picture Show*, a movie set in a nineteen-fifties crumbling, bleak, dust-blown West Texas town which is slowly dying, economically and spiritually.

It wasn't always this way here, however. At the dawn of the twentieth-century, McLean was coming into its own as a center for agriculture and oil. The town really took off in nineteen twenty-seven with the arrival of the *Mother Road.*

Route 66 cut right through the center of town and what followed was a flood of visitors who needed to gas up, be fed, entertained, and housed. The money rolled in. The population quickly trebled to two thousand. Churches sprang up. There was a bank and a newspaper. Restaurants and filling stations were situated on every corner of town, their skinned and twisted skeletal remains evidence of that today. During World War Two, a prisoner of war camp was built just outside town for three thousand captured Germans, generating buckets of federal dollars.

The good times ran into a brick wall with the coming of the *I-40*, which is just one mile from the center of McLean, but it just may as well be one hundred, or one million.

There's little evidence of actual life today in McLean. Driving slowly through the center of town, and pulling over now and then to take a few photographs, I don't see a single person and it's mid-morning on a weekday. The library is closed, as is the small museum dedicated to the glory days of *Route 66.* I do see a light burning behind the frosted window of some small business so I assume someone's in there, and through the closed doors of a machine shop I hear metal grinding on metal. Two cars are parked in front of the *Cactus Inn*, so maybe it's accepting guests. The Senior Center and the two antique shops are closed. The art deco *Avalon* movie house is boarded up, as are the bookend restaurants.

I make a second loop of the town and finally spot

someone—an old man coming out of a small building carrying a fat burlap bag, which he tosses into the bed of a nineteen-sixties black *Ford* pickup.

I pull up alongside the truck and use a tried-and-true opening to get people talking.

"Hi. Can you please tell me if there's any place to grab a bite to eat around here?"

The man laughs. "You can right near starve to death if you expect to find a restaurant here anymore."

He's a tall, handsome, ramrod straight, clean-shaven man of around eighty, with a weathered face and full head of gray hair, looking quite at home in a pair of vintage overalls pulled up over a nicely-ironed white, long sleeve shirt.

"Nearest place I can think of is maybe over in Shamrock," he says. "Can't guarantee nothing, though. Been a while now since I was over that way. Maybe you can pick up something at the little gas station store around the corner there. It should be open."

I step from the car, introduce myself and we shake hands. His is a huge, gnarled hand, a hand which has been around.

"How's it going?" I ask.

"Well, any day I wake up I consider a good day, or at least the start to one," he says, smiling. "No telling how it'll end, not that I'd actually want to know."

A droopy-eyed dog stirs from behind the stack of burlap bags and gives me the once over. Seeing nothing of interest, the old hound retreats from view.

"That's Homer. Turned fourteen not long ago. He can't do much of anything these days, but he's still pretty good company for an old man like me. In his prime he was sure something to see. Loved to swim in the pond down by my neighbors spread when it got really hot. When he'd not show up at home, I could usually find him down there, swimming, chasing rabbits. The only time he chases rabbits now is in his sleep."

I state the obvious. "Sure looks pretty quiet around here this morning."

"Can't get much quieter, I guess," he answers with a smile. "But that's not necessarily a bad thing if you think about it. Too much going on has a way of sometimes tempting folks into doing what they shouldn't be doing."

He walks around the truck and adjusts the positioning of some of the burlap bags he had already deposited there. "Time was when this place was teeming," he continues. "Course that was long ago. Not much going on at all around here now, as you can rightly see."

"Doesn't that make you a little sad?"

"The way I see it, pretty much everything has a limited time on earth. McLean just reached its limit. If you look at it that way, then it's not so bad. If you see it as natural, then it isn't all that threatening, if you know what I mean."

"I take it you've lived around here for a while?"

"All my life 'cepting a few years back during Korea."

"The Korean War?"

"I was too young to fight the Japs, but old enough to get in my licks when Korea got going good. I was just seventeen when the big war was finishing up in the Pacific. I wanted to go bad but my daddy made me wait. He told me if I was anxious to fight, somebody would eventually stir up a ruckus and I'd get my war. He was right. He usually was, but when I was over in that snow with a million screaming Chinamen charging at me, I wished he were wrong."

He leans back against the truck, legs crossed. The old dog slowly rises and plops its huge head on the man's shoulder.

"Homer, you lazy thing, you," he laughs. "I do love this dog.

Can't imagine his not being around. Then, of course, he could outlive me."

"What was it like here back in the forties and fifties? Had to be way different."

"Oh, lots of people around, that's for sure. Plenty of easy money, and no shortage of people chasing after it. No end of pretty girls around to tempt a young man either."

He gestures up the street. "Met my Lorraine on the corner there. That's where I first laid eyes on her. Most beautiful girl I ever did see. I knew right then and there she was all I wanted out of life. Things happened fast for us. Marriage, children. Fifty-two years flew by just like that. Lorraine passed on ten months ago."

"I'm sorry to hear that."

"Fine woman," he says softly. "She was the best any man could ever hope for. Her daddy owned a spread over near Amarillo and she knew pretty much everything there was to know about ranching. We started small, built things up over time. We had a fine life together, even when times were tough, and there were plenty of them for sure...We never did get to town all that much. Never had much of a reason to, 'ceptin' to pick up special necessaries at the store, and we'd take in a motion picture show now and then. Lorraine was a big fan of all those romance pictures, but I was able to coax her to a good old western from time to time by promising to take her out to dinner afterwards." The old man smiles at the memory.

"When did the theater close?"

"Can't rightly say I remember. Long time ago is all I know. I tend to lose track of time and stuff like that more and more these days. Likely 'cause there's more of it to remember and getting old doesn't make remembering things any easier to begin with. Time just doesn't seem all that important anymore, at least ways to me."

I look at the deserted sidewalks and empty streets. "Must say I'm surprised at just how quiet it is around here is this morning. It always like this?"

"Pretty much," he answers. "McLean went downhill real fast when all that traffic stopped coming through the center of town. That was about twenty-five, thirty years ago. When the traffic dried up so did pretty much everything else around here."

"That couldn't have been easy."

"All I know for sure those times are gone now, and will never return, at least not so I'll ever see it happen. Oh, from time to time I think about the old days, old friends, faces no longer around; the way it used to be here...Lorraine's passing hit me real hard. I guess you could rightly say it cut the heart out of me. Left me pretty much with nothing more to do but wait around for my time to join her. Problem is it's sure taking its own sweet time."

The old man looks up at the rolling clouds and electrically-charged sky, picks up Homer and places the dog in the front seat of the truck.

"Weather changes fast, especially this time of the year," he says.

I help him tie down a blue plastic tarp over the burlap bags.

A clap of thunder, a surging wind, and a sideways burst of stinging rain sends us scurrying for our vehicles. The man and I wave our goodbyes through slapping windshield wipers as we drive off in opposite directions.

Entry 12: Chewing up pavement at a furious clip. Not much to see around here—barren, colorless flatlands—so am anxious to get on down the road.

Slam on the brakes when I spot a small wooden marker off to the side of the two-lane country road. It's rare I allow one to pass unread. There's a wealth of history revisited in those markers and I don't want to miss out on anything.

Good thing I stopped. This particular one informs in brevity of words I've reached the Continental Divide. The actual spine of the North American continent. Bob Seger wrote about it in a song. Pop in the CD every morning when I hit the road. Refuse to drive even a mile without the pulsating beat coursing through my veins and lyrics filling my head with uplifting notions.

A man standing beside his two-wheeler looking out at the Divide, feeling free, soul rising like a hawk, he could go east, he could go west, it was all up to him to decide...

That aside, I really could have done without learning the Continental Divide is a drainage ditch. A glorified drainage ditch, but still a drainage ditch—an imaginary line running along a continuous ridge of mountain summits which divide the continent into two primary drainage areas. Knowledge can be such a buzz kill.

I straddle the line as everyone surely does, and allow my mind free rein over the weighty implications of this very spot of earth. Water poured into the ground by my left foot flows to the Pacific Ocean, water by my right foot will eventually reach the Atlantic coastline or Gulf of Mexico. Maybe even Hudson Bay.

I debate taking a leak on both sides of the Divide, just to see if it would actually flow off in multiple directions, but decide that wouldn't be classy. Besides, someone in the Indian gift shop across the road might see me, although there are no cars parked in front of the place, and I could probably get away with a quick wiz. But *quick* and *wiz* are really not words which belong together in the same sentence at my age, and I don't feel like hanging out for the time it would take to complete the mission.

The desert wind suddenly kicks up and the air turns bitingly cold. Happens that way above seven-thousand feet, even in summer. I put on a jacket and look to the north, over a vast, rolling yellow plain towards the Colorado Rockies, hidden just over the horizon. I feel a sense of elation at reaching here, even though it is quite by accident and without forethought, which is quickly becoming a hallmark of the way I travel. Plan little, slide along in blissful ignorance, but seize the moment when it presents itself.

Before moving on, I declare this ditch the "official" launch pad of my journey into the heart of the American Southwest, a wilderness of muscular mountains, rugged canyons, red rock cliffs, high broad basins, volcanic landscapes, deserts, grasslands...the ancestral home of the Apache, Comanche, Navajo, Hopi, Paiute...

Entry 13: The setting sun found me bent over the steering wheel trying to relieve pressure on my aching back and butt, as I took dead aim on the western horizon, determined to put a few more miles behind me before finally surrendering and pulling over for the night.

As I roll down the country road in the gathering darkness, the flat, dull landscape unveils specks of lights from distant ranch houses. The first stars appear. The Milky Way soon takes command of the sky. The car lights pick up the eyes of night creatures on the prowl near the road. Way off to the left, soaring thunderheads spewing great streams of lightning. Straight ahead, and close, a halo of white light builds fast in front of me. Sure sign of people.

I soon find myself in a small town. It's Sunday night and traffic is practically non-existent. A few pickup trucks, a shirtless guy on a motor scooter. The main drag narrows as I move through town. Not much to see. Closed businesses, boarded up buildings, sand swirling across the road. A small group of teenagers hanging out on a street corner give me the once over as I drive by. I'm careful to keep at the twenty mile per hour limit to avoid becoming a speed trap victim. This place looks like it can really use the money my fine would generate.

Stop at a convenience store and pick up a two buck *Saran*-wrapped ham and cheese sandwich and a bottle of water for dinner, which I wolf down as I gas up the car. It doesn't take long for my stomach to express its displeasure.

Pull into the first motel I come across. The neon sign's dark and parking lot empty so I'm not even sure this rundown survivor from the nineteen-fifties is open for business. Then I see someone stirring in the office, silhouetted against a weak light bulb.

Twenty-four dollars secures me a room with no view, along with a lumpy mattress, a deeply-stained tub, a toilet with a semi-detached seat, a wheezing, dripping window air conditioner. The walls are dirty. Once white, now yellow. The smell of ancient mold hovers in the air. Mouse turds congregate in a corner of the room. A bare light bulb hangs from the ceiling. The shade to the bedside lamp has scorch marks and the white pine night table has burns from unattended cigarettes. The TV reception is snowy and limited to a few stations broadcasting from someplace far away.

While most people would probably howl at the condition

of the room and bolt, it really doesn't matter all that much to me. I'm no stranger to Third World shitholes so places like this don't normally cause me to wince. In fact, to my conditioned world view, the room is quite okay for what I have in mind for it. A few hours' sleep, then hit the road again. Quick in, quick out. Not even enough time for the bedbugs to settle in for a decent meal.

I didn't expect a knock at the door. It's the woman from the front desk and she's carrying a six-pack of *Budweiser*. "Drinks on the house," she grins.

"Well, actually," I stammer, "I'm kind of planning an early..."

She isn't to be denied. Brushes right by me and takes a seat on the end of the bed. She pops open a beer and thrusts it at me.

She's good-natured enough so I accept the beer and take a seat in a rickety rush-seat chair by the door, which I keep open to allow the swirling gusts of wind from the approaching storm to take a bite out of the stench.

My uninvited guest is a full-figured, plain-looking woman of about forty, no makeup, broad face with sharp features, pitch-black eyes, and long, gray-streaked raven hair pulled back into a ponytail. Native American, for sure.

Introduces herself as Mai. Tells me it means flower. It can also mean bright, as in colorful.

I quickly learn her late husband inherited the motel five years earlier from his uncle, a World War Two veteran who lost a leg and an eye on Saipan. They immediately gave up their dead-end jobs at a chicken farm and moved into the "owner's quarters," an old, single-wide trailer parked out back behind the laundry room.

Her husband was white, a journeyman farm hand with big

dreams and she latched on to him partly as a way to escape the grinding poverty of the Reservation. Their hope was to one day buy a small ranch, but it wasn't in the cards. Just couldn't raise the twenty-five percent down payment for a piece of property no matter how hard they tried.

"Bankers don't much like people like us," Mai says. "They want to deal with lily whites who know which forks to use at fancy dinner parties out at the *Country Club.* Not much of a place, if you ask me, not that I have much experience being around them. Used to deliver chickens to the restaurant there a while back. Wasn't impressed by nothing I saw there. A lot of people putting on airs, if you ask me."

Mai opens another beer and hands it to me.

I'm already light-headed from the brew, fatigue, and high altitude. Feel a chill and rub my arms. I'm amazed how dramatically the temperature fluctuates out in the desert. I've heard about it all my life. To experience it is quite something else. Twenty degrees in way less than one hour, I guess, and it's still dropping, but I don't want to close the door as long as she's here.

Mai: "Things were going along for us as well as could be expected, I guess, given the circumstances, till my husband took up the bottle. Harvey's spirit was pretty well broken by all the bad things thrown at him in life and it all just came together at one time, and he vanished. That was July year before last. No one around here's seen him since and no one has any idea where he might be. Search parties from the sheriff's office went looking for him out in the desert, but found nothing. Big surprise there," she says sarcastically. "If he doesn't show up soon, then the court will declare him dead. If you ask me, I think that poor man just got drunk and wandered off into the desert and died. Maybe heat stroke, snake bite, fell, or something like that. Hopefully, someone will stumble on his remains one day and the mystery will be solved and he can get a proper burial. He deserves at least that."

"You planning on staying around here then?" I ask.

"I don't have much choice, do I? Oh, it's not really all that bad of a life here if you don't mind being poor, bored, and living in the middle of a desert." She laughs at her predicament and in the process sucks some beer up her nose, which only makes her laugh harder.

Mai recovers her composure and asks, "So, what's going on in the outside world?"

I tell her she's not missing much.

"This economy sure isn't doing anybody any good," she says. "TV's been doing some things about small towns and all the trouble they're in. Places just like right here, only it's twice as bad as they say. Business has really fallen off bad the last year or so. People just aren't traveling so much anymore, not with four dollar gas, and when they do they're real tight with how they spend. Here, we usually only get locals looking to get it on over weekends, some bikers, and a few people like yourself, half who probably wandered off the highway and couldn't figure how to get back to it in the dark. I barely break even some months, but expenses aren't all that much. This place was already free and clear when we inherited it. Thank God for that!"

She smiles as she looks around the room. "Guess you noticed by now upkeep here's not a big expense."

"Oh, it's not so bad. There's a lot worse places out there, believe me."

Mai laughs. "Heavens, I hate to think where you've been!"

Mai can trace her family tree all the way back to the late-seventeen hundreds. Great grandfather was a cavalry scout.

She came off the Reservation to attend junior college. Nearly finished the first year, but her grandmother fell ill so she returned home, took a job at a convenience store at minimum wage, and dreamed of what could have been.

"I once thought some about teaching. That would have been a nice life and I could have maybe made a contribution, maybe improved things some. This place could sure use that."

She excuses herself when an old *Plymouth* mini-van pulls into the parking lot. It's packed with Spanish-speaking men, seven or eight of them, all with downcast eyes, looking uncomfortable and out of place. Some money changes hands and they pile into rooms a few doors down from mine.

Mai returns a minute later carrying a fresh six-pack and parks herself at the end of the bed. "Mexicans," she says. "Most likely illegals being escorted to some place back east, or up north. Heard the *Coyotes* are getting two, three thousand a head, maybe more. The Mexicans coming through are not bad people," she adds. "Just trying to get by pretty much like the rest of us."

It's raining now, great sheets of it sweeping across the parking lot. I decide to close the door. Mai pulls back the lid on a beer can and the spray reaches my pillow.

Mai: "Hard to say who's in worse shape—the illegals, or Indians around these parts. My grandmother lives in a little community out in the middle of nowhere. Just a bunch of small cinderblock houses, and when I say *nowhere*, I mean *nowhere*. No trees to speak of. Hot, cold, dry, nothing ever going on. I get her a little money when I can to help her get by. It's never much, but it's all I can swing. You ever been to a reservation, the real part, not the glittery part you find on the big highways, places with fancy casinos?"

"Not yet, but I'm hoping to."

"Let me tell you, medical care's terrible out there. Most people can't find work, and them that do are paid hardly nothing, and what they do make is often wasted on whiskey. That poison killed my daddy. Mother died when I was three giving birth to my brother. He died a week later. I've always said the baby could have been saved had he been anyplace else. People could sure use some help out there, but no one ever really listens, except maybe during election times and the promises made then are hardly ever kept afterwards. Maybe my people should take a few scalps." She laughs at the thought. "Now that for sure would get someone's attention."

There's a loud noise on the street. A sharp *crack*, and close. Mai looks out the door, and quickly returns to her perch and shrugs. "Don't know what that was all about, but it's smart to at least check. You never know when some fool drunk with a six-shooter takes it into his head to even a score, or celebrate a birth, or some such thing. Couple times a year someone gets hurt bad like that."

She holds out another beer.

"No, thanks. I'm afraid one more would knock me out cold. I'm nearly there already."

Mai laughs. "Being out cold in a town like this is better than being stone sober."

I take the beer.

She presses on, reminiscing about growing up...

"You know, I never saw a rose, a real rose, till I was nearly grown. Cactus roses, yes, but never one with petals that felt so silky when you rubbed them against your skin...I was probably eight or nine before I saw a color TV or rode in a car, other than my grandfather's old pickup, which didn't run most of the time anyway...I was sick and tired of everything by the time I was a teenager. Angry all the time. Just wanted to go, although

I had no place to go to...I guess I'm one of the lucky ones who managed to get out, although you may not think of this place as being lucky, or getting out."

Mai kicks off her shoes, stretches out full-length on the bed, and starts in on another beer.

I manage a few hours' sleep before sunrise, and revive myself with a time-wasting shower, in no particular hurry because I've come to realize this day, like all other days, is wide open to whatever I can cook up, without constraints of time, or the need to consider the wants and needs of others.

This feeling is most potent at the break of day when the body is fresh, when harnessed energy demands to be unleashed. The hunger to be somewhere else is a constant and irrepressible companion, and I alone control the pace and flow, when I kick it into high gear and the wheels roll.

I step out into the parking lot. The Mexicans' mini-van has left. Mai's nowhere to be seen. Across the lot, a lone biker's wiping down his *Harley* with a towel.

The sun's climbed high by now and the bright light reflecting off the concrete has me reaching for my sunglasses.

Entry 14: Brushing up on my outdoor vocabulary. Out here, the challenge of knowing where you're standing and what you're seeing is ratcheted up by a blizzard of alien names attached to surface features, so I decide to buff-up one word at a time.

Butte is the word I hear spoken most when it relates to topography, so it's the logical starting point. Now pay close attention. They'll be a quiz later.

A butte is an isolated hill or mountain with steep slopes and a flat top. It's first cousin to a mesa, an isolated relatively flat-topped natural elevation usually more extensive that a butte and less extensive than a plateau which, by the way, is a land area having a relatively level surface raised sharply above adjacent land on at least one side. Some people call it a table-top. Got all that?

I pretty much now call everything a butte and forget about mesas unless I'm absolutely convinced the top sizes are significantly different, not always easy to determine from a distance. I find myself using the words interchangeably when hanging out with tourists from east of the Mississippi. They don't know shit anyway and I enjoy sounding like an expert. They eat it up.

The next word on my study list: *hogback.*

Entry 15: The spreading Navajo Willow catches my eye, rising high like it does above a sea of dry scrub along this all but forgotten stretch of *Route 66*. A fine place to take a break.

The tree is at least fifty feet tall, its green symmetrical crown providing some shade from the murderous sun, the heat mitigated only slightly by a feeble breeze limping in from the north.

The willow stands watch over the remains of what I suspect is an early country store which catered to cross-country travelers of at least a half century ago. Not much is left of the place now but the two side walls. The roof has caved in, taking out the façade and rear wall. The only solid clue I have this had probably once been a store are the faded words *Cold Beer* painted in red on the exterior of the east-facing wall.

There's what I think is an outhouse off to the side, the rotted wood planks leaning heavily to the right and ready to give way. Nearly overlook the two wooden crosses some twenty-five yards behind the structure, barely visible in the tall grass. I investigate. Nothing written on the primitive crosses. Just pieces of dried out lumber hammered together. God only knows what that's all about.

Intrigues me every time I stumble on one of these places, and they're not in short supply out here. I want to know who built them and what they did when they ultimately gave up on what had certainly been their dream of a better life and moved on, *if* they moved on.

There's no one around now to answer such questions. Time has simply erased all records of these people which, when I think about it, is pretty much the fate of each and every one of us.

Entry 16: I love food. I indulge often, sometimes five, six times a day, and I'm not overly particular about what I eat. If it's not twitching, gasping for air, or staring back at me, down it goes. There are a few exceptions, of course. I can't imagine eating a spider, for example, or any dish containing the word blood, tongue, or testicle.

I had such high hopes when I set out on this road trip across America. All that wonderful regional food of legend waiting for me. But it didn't take long to realize the open road these days is pretty much a culinary wasteland.

There is sameness to the food, a blandness that excites neither the eye, nor nose, nor palate. It's more than likely pre-cooked, wrapped in plastic, frozen, microwaved, and served on paper or plastic plates, or in *Styrofoam* containers.

There was a time when one could readily identify a geographic region by the food served, but in this homogeneous society, where a restaurant chain hamburger in Blacksburg, Virginia, tastes identical to one in Elk City, Oklahoma, that's hard to find.

I quickly discovered the last line of defense against the

detestable culinary erosion are those independent family restaurants and diners one stumbles on now and then...rare little jewels where the food crackles with personality, often cooked by sweaty, unshaven men in t-shirts with cigarettes dangling from their lips.

Breakfast is ones best bet to be fed reasonably well. Served up are fresh jumbo eggs cooked to order, and sizzling thick-sliced bacon, crispy fried potatoes, steaming grits, light and fluffy pancakes and waffles. In fact, as this road trip progresses, breakfast is fast becoming my “main meal” of the day.

While the American *table* is in dire straits, I take some comfort in knowing there are still places on this planet where people are actually keeping culinary faith with their ancestors, although the fast food intrusion is making major inroads just about every place you go.

One notable exception—Tonga—out in the far reaches of the South Pacific, an island tropical paradise along the International Dateline. Actually, the Dateline would have cut straight through the island chain but for the King of Tonga who decreed it be diverted slightly to the west of the islands so his kingdom would be more closely linked to his Polynesian neighbors to the east on Fiji and Tahiti, and not his darker-skinned Melanesian neighbors to the west, on places like Guadalcanal and New Guinea. Look at the Dateline on a map. Where it abruptly jogs to the left and then back again is where you’ll find Tonga.

The population of one hundred thousand is spread out over seven hundred thousand square kilometers of ocean on several hundred islands.

Tonga somehow avoided formal colonization, pretty much the only place in the South Pacific to do so, which accounts for its purity of soul and spirit, untainted by colonial infrastructure and architecture, and predictable food.

I'd flown into Tonga to report on a meaningless news story to anyone outside the immediate region, and probably not even there. I'd been owed a favor by my boss, and this was payback. Took three changes of aircraft to get there and the flights droned on forever.

The *boondoggle* gave me a chance to see a new region, catch a little beach time in paradise, clear my head, and wash off the stench of war. I make no apologies for my actions. I'd been covering mayhem non-stop for months and considered this a well-deserved reward, or so I convinced myself.

While I rarely made it to the actual "news" events which commanded my presence, it was no accident I never missed a meal.

The Tongan culture is truly food-centric and the people who call this island chain home go out of their way to make sure we invited foreign guests want for nothing.

The highlight of the trip is a moonlit luau on a sandy beach cove under, of course, swaying palms. Included on the menu is pig served up every which way, along with baked mahi-mahi, purple yams, banana bread, guava cake, and so forth. Pretty much the same menu served at mainline hotel luau's on Waikiki Beach, but without all the tourists and annoying ukulele music.

Where the Tongans' luau veers off into culinary *Minerva* is when blackened squid is laid before me on a palm frond. I'm hesitant at first. Who can possibly blame me? This concoction is rotting squid rings dumped into a vat of bubbling coconut oil and topped with a thick, black sauce of unknown origin, at least to me.

My hosts look at me expectantly. I can see faint smiles forming. They've obviously been here before and have seen outsiders go pale, or worse, at the prospect of putting one of those uninviting rings into their mouths. I wasn't about to give them the satisfaction of seeing me buckle under pressure, so I take a stab at it.

The dish is, well, magnificent! Unlike anything I've eaten before, or since. I still wake up nights thinking of it. I tried once to duplicate it in my kitchen, but failed miserably. There were times I was tempted to return to Tonga just to recreate the moment, but realized it likely wouldn't be the same. It seldom is. Hold tight, I say, to comforting memories and don't risk screwing them up by thinking you can reach out and recapture the past. There lurk life's most disappointing moments.

The very *worst* dish came in a place which didn't surprise me at all—South Korea. My apologies to the people of the Korean Peninsula, but I've long considered the native food to be the absolute pits, and the pit of all pits was spread out before me one night in Seoul.

The city had just won rights to host the Summer Olympics and I'd flown over from my home base in Tokyo to report on the celebrations. The head of Seoul Olympic Committee took me out for a night on the town, no expense spared, and dinner included every single Korean dish I could possibly despise, and then some. There's kimchee, of course, a staple at every meal over there and an insult to the humble cabbage. Next served is fermented skate, followed in quick succession by boiled intestine sausage, raw crabs, and chicken feet. Then the meal took a turn for the worse, which I didn't think was possible. Served up is my very own block of a pale, quivering gelatin substance and buried inside, clearly visible, is a giant sea slug. It's at least the size of my thumb, green-brown in color, and very much alive, squirming around in its tomb, desperately looking for an exit which doesn't exist.

While the other guests are preoccupied chomping down on

their slugs, I stealthy extract *mine* from the gelatin with a butter knife, wrap it in a napkin and place it in my pocket, with the intent to return it to some as yet determined body of water the following morning where, I hope, it can live out a long life in its natural environment.

Sadly, the slug fails to survive the night in my hotel room wash basin, but I'm at least able to partly complete my mission. I manage to return the little guy to water.

I flush it down the toilet.

Entry 17: Bouncing all over the map. Zigzagging every which way. Pretty much no rhyme or reason to any of it. Just following my nose. I'm starting to hit my stride. Much more comfortable now, more willing to take risks. Energy level's certainly up. Racking up the miles at a furious clip. Seeing much. Time's flying by. Losing track of the actual day of the week, as if knowing that really matters. Taking it from moment to moment. Dazzled by the majestic scenery. Visually overpowering. Can't take enough photos. The sense of freedom's staggering.

Entry 18: I hate trucks and it's pretty clear there's no love lost for me either.

No type of truck escapes my wrath. Eighteen-wheelers, dump trucks, flatbeds, tankers, cement mixers, wide loads, tow trucks, refrigeration trucks, car carriers, delivery trucks, box trucks, garbage carriers, pickups with monster wheels, trucks hauling tanks, prefabs, earth-movers, logs, quarry rock, hazardous materials, carnival rides, chickens, lipstick, buttermilk...

They're always crowding in close, lording over me with their size advantage. I can be blissfully cruising along, minding my own business, a vast open highway cutting through the high desert stretched out before me, admiring the last light of day playing off a majestic string of distant mountains, a buttery moon on the rise, then comes the ambush. It's quick and well-executed. There's nowhere to run, no place to hide, no time to react.

The trucks arrive all at once and, in military precision, take up strategic positions around me in an ever-tightening encirclement, so close and so intimate I can reach out and stroke the armored flanks of the beast, now a singular creature with a common pulse.

I remain trapped there, sometimes for what seems like an eternity, pounded and buffeted, staggering under the onslaught, unable to escape.

There's a conspiracy involved, of course. Don't ask me how I know. I just do. I'm convinced trucks actually lie in wait for me, parked with motors running at rest stops, weigh stations, and highway on-ramps, and when I pass the attack is launched.

Trucks to the left off me, trucks to the right of me, trucks fore and aft, and me stuck in the middle of the rolling, unholy alliance, the sun blocked out, road signs and billboards obscured, whole towns and even cities passed through without my realizing it, lungs seared and eyes burning from diesel fumes, fearful the road litter of nails, tin cans, moose cadavers, broken tailpipes, horseshoes, brooms, crutches, rakes, pitchforks, vacuum cleaners, satellite dishes, and microwave ovens will have their way with me, all the while terrified a man-size chunk of shrapnel from a blown truck tire will shatter the windshield and deposit itself in my lap.

In such tight quarters it is absolutely imperative to keep focused, with both hands on the steering wheel at all times. Switching radio channels is out, as are answering or placing cell phone calls, eating, drinking, daydreaming, coughing, and sneezing. Most of all sneezing! At high speed, a lot of ground can be covered in the life-span of an everyday sneeze and, in such tight quarters, those few seconds when the eyes are forced shut as the sneeze erupts in final fury, can be the margin between living and dying.

Entry 19: Stop for dinner at a truck stop way out in the *sticks*. Really don't want to but I'm hungry and there's nothing else around but fast food crud and I'm not up to that tonight, not that the alternative holds out much promise.

A classic *greasy spoon*. Flickering and spitting fluorescent lights, a racket of rattling pots and pans intruding on the dining area, kitchen staff embroiled in a loud argument, chipped plastic plates, bent cutlery, smell of stale coffee and road sweat. More flies than customers.

"So, where you from, buddy?"

I look up from my bowl of chili, swivel on the counter stool, and make eye contact with the scary-looking guy in the booth a few feet away.

He repeats the question. He seems friendly enough so I relax, but only slightly. Learned long ago to stay on guard around tattooed strangers with necks twice the size of mine.

"Ah, North Carolina."

"Know it well. Nice roads," he says matter-of-factly.

This is a giant of a man, his body claiming most of the real estate on his side of the red vinyl booth. He invites me to join him.

"I hate eating alone," he says, "and I like company. I meet all kinds of interesting people in this job. You interesting, buddy?"

Good question. I thought I may have been at one time. Not so sure now. I'd have to mull that one over. I shrug and join him.

Tells me his name is Bobby. Guess his age at somewhere in the mid-forties. Bald with a neatly-trimmed goatee. Weighs close to three hundred if he's not there already. Still, he looks to be in pretty good shape. Arms decorated with tattoos. I spot a ship's bell and anchor, and what appears to be a mermaid. No-brainer which branch of the military he served in.

A skinny waitress with red-rimmed eyes and swimming in a faded orange uniform trimmed with white lace brings Bobby's order. Meatloaf, which she promises was freshly-made today, along with sides of mashed potatoes, buttered cabbage, black-eyed peas, a wedge of corn bread, a slice of lemon meringue pie, along with a boxed to-go order of even more pie.

"You boys need anything else, you just holler, okay?"

"I can always use a little more sweet tea, sweet thing," he says, pointing at his half-empty glass.

She smiles that waitress smile we all recognize. "Be right back, good-looking."

My dinner companion was born, raised and lived in some Kentucky town I'd never heard of. Bobby says he's been driving a truck since two thousand three. Before that, worked as second shift foreman in a small factory which padlocked its gates when it could no longer compete with foreign imports.

"Town went to hell in a hand basket after that," he adds. "No jobs, downtown fell apart. Stores that had been there forever, back to my granddaddy's time, went out of business. Broke everyone's heart seeing it all go down like that. A hundred years of history, people's lives, wiped out in a second. Some folks found work at the *Target* over in Jeffersontown, but for me the pay wasn't worth the gas it took to get there and back."

Bobby's married to a woman named Joyce he's known since junior high, and they have three kids, all boys, now teenagers.

Bobby volunteers he cleared just over forty-four thousand dollars last year.

"Not much money, but in these hard times I suppose I'm lucky to have work," he says matter-of-factly. "Don't get home near often enough, not working sixty, seventy, sometimes eighty hours a week. At least the health insurance ain't all that bad. That actually keeps me doing what I'm doing. We'd be screwed without it. Joyce was diagnosed with breast cancer two years ago. She's okay now, I guess, but the medical bills were through the roof. While insurance didn't cover all of it, it at least kept us out of the poor house, although I had to take out a small second mortgage to cover our share. Be some time paying that off."

The waitress returns with a full pitcher of tea, which she sets on the table. "You boys look thirsty, so thought you might like to have this."

"Thanks," he says. "Appreciate you looking after us like this."

"Us working folks need to stick together," she smiles.

After she leaves, Bobby asks me to remind him to leave a nice tip. "She works as hard as any of us, maybe harder. Bet she has a house full of kids to support and no man around to help. I see people like her all the time. She looks fifty, but I'd bet she's no more than thirty, thirty-five. She sure as hell never thought it would turn out the way it has, but I guess most of us can say that."

I quiz Bobby about what life's like for a trucker out on the road.

He rolls his eyes. "Between cops hassling us about speeding and weight, tires and other stuff, and trying to avoid idiots in cars just begging to be crushed under my wheels, it ain't romantic like song writers have made it out to be. Let them spend one week behind the wheel of my rig and they'll be singing a different tune real quick...My body's all beat to hell from the hard miles I've put on it out on the road, and the sleep I'm missing sure ain't doing me no good at all. At this rate, I'll be lucky to make it to fifty."

Bobby wants to know why I'm so far from home. "Vacation, or something?"

I explain the road trip, the decision-making process, the execution.

Bobby's eyes go wide. "You mean you're doing this voluntarily?! Man, I'd eat a bucket of lizard shit to be able to spend every night with the family, to never go more than twenty miles from home, but I guess not every one of us is that way. Some people just got the *itch*. I've seen it before. Lots of truckers out on the road got it, and that's one itch that's hard to scratch."

Bobby takes a bite of his pie and looks through the dirty plate glass window out into the parking lot and the sea of trucks there and shakes his head.

"Don't you just hate bitchin' summer nights when it never seems to get dark? I'd like to pullover and get some quick shut-eye, just a few minutes, but I could never sleep when it was light, even a little bit, so I just keep on rolling. Dropping off my load in Fort Smith tomorrow, and will be back home late, if I'm lucky, but I'll have to haul ass to do it."

Entry 20: Today's the anniversary of my death. Quite an accomplishment to live to tell about, if you ask me.

Eleven years this very day, but it seems like yesterday. Every detail still vivid, and haunting. I tend to relive it more than I should, but I just can't seem to park it somewhere and forget about it. I suppose that's to be expected. After all, coming back from the dead tends to stick with a person.

It began at three in the morning. A mild tightness in my chest. A buzzing feeling in my throat. The sweats. No pain, however. Don't worry, I tell myself. Maybe it's indigestion. That pepperoni pizza last night. Or maybe I'm just tired. Not as young as I once was. Not by a long shot. More sleep will fix things. That always works. Besides, I don't want to wake up my girlfriend without a very good reason.

Things escalate...

A siren. Faint at first, then louder, finally screaming. The sensation of movement. I open my eyes. Hovering over me is a young man holding a pair of paddles just above my chest. He's smiling, looking relieved.

"You use those things on me?" I know the answer but ask anyway. Asking questions is what I do.

"If I have to, I'll first give you a sedative."

It's bullshit, but I accept what he says because it's what I want to hear. Not to accept it would trigger far too many negative scenarios, and I had enough of those already bouncing around in my head.

Next. Gurney wheels clicking on a tile floor. Lift my head from the pillow. At the end of the dimly-lit corridor stand a tightly-clustered group of people looking in my direction. A curtain is pulled back. Bright lights now. I'm rolled into a small, antiseptic room and immediately surrounded by people in white, maybe a dozen in all, each moving with practiced precision.

Objects are attached to my legs, stomach and chest. Tubing crisscrosses my body. A pill is slid under my tongue. I'm fed oxygen. The young doctor studies the green-screened bank of monitors, frowns, and shakes her head. I wish I hadn't seen her do that. A nurse with a clipboard sits on a stool at the end of the bed taking notes. The EMT from my ride here looks through the curtain and says something to the doctor. Someone asks how I feel. I don't remember answering. I try to transport myself someplace else. Someplace gentle and kind, but the moment refuses to release me. I feel tears on my cheeks. Warm and slow-moving. An older woman with a kind face is holding my hand.

"I don't want to be here," I whisper.

Then nothing.

I'm told my heart stopped beating three times that morning.

My assorted deaths passed unnoticed by me. I didn't see them coming, or see them going. I didn't levitate in the emergency room and look down on the frantic efforts to save my life. There's no white light beckoning me. My father and grandparents do not appear through a mist to escort me into a new and better world. There's no awareness. Not even blackness.

That disappoints me to this very day. I'd always held out hope there was something to look forward to after my time on earth, but I now suspected all I had was this life and this life alone. *Not* such a good thing to know.

Entry 21: Today drove through a stretch of desert flatlands. Taking my time. Off to the right, faraway, lands forms shimmering in the noon day heat. In every direction, a sweep of red sand decorated with stunted cacti.

The road ahead is deserted. Nothing in the rear-view mirror but the company of my own shadow. An open bag of *Cheetos Puffs* and a crumbled *Snickers* wrapper's on the seat beside me. A three-hour-old dollar ice tea from *McDonald's* occupies the center cup holder, the remaining contents rocking back and forth, keeping time with the subtle dips and waves in the road. CD player's kicking out Springsteen.

I could say the landscape around here looks like a nuclear

battlefield, but that would be minimizing the view. Not much evidence of life, at least life I can see. And so dry. Heard when locals speak of a three-inch rain, they mean three inches *between* drops. Mark Twain said it was his experience the thermometer here stays at one hundred twenty all the time—except when it goes higher.

Arizona. Interesting place. Think I just may hang around for a while.

Entry 22: Stood high on Blue Mesa looking out at what was once a vast, fertile floodplain crisscrossed by rivers and streams, the banks lined with stately conifer trees...a land ruled by crocodile-like reptiles, giant amphibians, vast herds of small dinosaurs, and leathery-winged pterosaurs.

The Petrified Forest looks very different today from the way it was two hundred million plus years ago. A desert now, and no insensate creatures on the prowl to speak of beyond irreverent tourists.

Millions of years of erosion have sculpted the badlands of blue, purple and green mudstones, mesas and buttes, into a stunning panorama unequaled anywhere else on earth.

This corner of the Painted Desert is rich with fields of petrified wood, surviving chunks, fragments and shavings of ancient trees uprooted and washed here by floods and buried by volcanic ash and sediment, the organic tissue long since replaced by brilliantly-colored quartz.

For some reason, I'd given no thought whatsoever to dropping by the Petrified Forest. It had just somehow slipped through the cracks when I first began going over the trip in my head way back when. Saw the sign for the national park on the highway and decided to take a look. Happy I made the time.

Check into a nearby motel. Low end, but so is everything

else around here. Pay ten days in advance. Get a nice discount off the day rate for the longer stay. Every dollar helps. Gas is eating me alive.

At sundown, drift into a bar on the main drag. Parking lot's nearly full so I suspect the beer is cold and the food halfway decent. Worth a try. Besides, not so many choices in a town this small.

Good crowd considering it's a Monday. Some Hispanics, mostly off in the darker corners keeping a low profile. A few bikers. Locals outnumber everyone.

Jukebox blaring. Country tunes along with a few standards. No *hip-hop* tolerated here. Beer's served in large glass mugs. Domestic brands only. The plastic menu's old, greasy and held together with tape. Cheeseburger with fries is four-fifty, a T-bone ten ninety-five.

Take a seat on a stool. Guy named Charlie's working behind the bar. It's his night job. He's a discount store assistant manager during the day. Charlie's a spare man with a pale complexion, and an *Adam's apple* the size of a baseball. Thirty-five-years-old, never really been anywhere, seen anything, and none of this bothers him in the least. In fact, he's proud of it, although he did tell me he'd one day like to make a trip to *Disney World* "just to see what the fuss is all about."

"I get down to Phoenix couple times a year to visit my sister," he says. "Everybody's always in a big hurry down there, all bent out of shape. Nope, I don't need that shit. The shit around here's good enough for me. It may not be great shit, but it's *my* shit...You may not know it looking at the place now, but this was an important cattle town a long time ago, and pretty wild. Big drives coming through all the time, gunfights in the streets and saloons, and stuff. That's when *I* should have lived, you know. Yes sir, real men back then. Not the pussy's you see everywhere today. Guys taking shit from their old ladies, being pushed around at work, being scared all the time."

Charlie goes to the kitchen when a bell rings and returns with the grilled cheese sandwich, coleslaw, and onion rings I ordered, along with a fresh beer, the overflow foam cascading down his arm and forming a frothy pool around my plate.

He then leans in close, speaking in a whisper now, sheepishly grinning from ear to ear. "If you're interested in a little action tonight, we got a place over on the North End that ain't half bad. My step-uncle runs it. Just tell him I sent you and he'll set you up real nice."

Later in the evening strike up a conversation with an older biker couple sitting at a nearby table. Names are Hank and Claire. They invite me to join them.

Surprised at the number of bikers I see on the road these days in my age group. Well-heeled, out of shape early-*Boomers* in factory-faded jeans and designer black leather jackets accompanied by *blue rinse* grandmothers occupying the rear touring seat, or occasionally a side car. They move solo down the road, or sometimes in caravans, slithering along like sidewinders. The sense of freedom they're experiencing is certainly seductive and there are times I wish I could join them, but just for short stretches. No way could I deal with an entire year on a motorcycle exposed to four season elements and sharing the road with trucks and distracted morons in cars. I shiver at the thought.

"Burnout, it was all about burnout!" Hank says emphatically. "Had to get out. Kids all grown and long since gone, time passing and nothing left to accomplish at work. It came down to now or never, and we chose *now*."

Claire: "I hired someone to manage my real estate business and moved my eldest daughter into the house to look after things while we're away. Hank bought the *Harley* and the rest is history. We've been rolling for ten weeks now, and lovin' it!"

Hank was an attorney in South Bend. Left behind the "corporate mentality and bullshit" when he turned sixty-three.

Hank's short in stature and rather portly. Claire's equally plump, but a head taller than her husband. Easy to tell she'd been a *looker* in her day. Maybe not a classic beauty, but a head-turner nonetheless.

"I had to get moving, or dry up and blow away," Hank says. "I needed to see something new and fresh. See if a sense of community still exists anywhere these days. Used to be we looked out for our neighbors, but not so much now. I see a scary future barreling down on us. Global warming, terrorists walking among us, those dick-heads in Washington doing nothing but spend, spend, spend. My kids and grandkids are sure going to pay a heavy price for the way we fucked things up. Some legacy, huh?! That's not so easy to live with."

A cop drops by the bar and takes away a young Hispanic in handcuffs. No show of any kind. Just a resignation on the part of the man who goes quietly, as if he were almost expecting this moment, or had experienced it before.

"Poor bastard," Hank says. "If we think we got it bad, all we got to do is look at those people. Squat waiting for them at home. Sending them back across the border accomplishes zilch. They're back again a week or two later. I say either seal up the border tight, or open it to all comers. It's practically that way now anyway."

Claire's face lights up when a Conway Twitty song kicks in on the jukebox. "Oh, I love that one!"

"I can almost hear the stillness as it yields to the sound of your heart beating..."

"I saw him perform once, you know," she adds. "Long time ago. Singing with his band on a long bed in a parking lot. Store opening of some kind, maybe. Something like that. A couple of guys in the crowd got into a big fight right there in front of him, but he just kept on singing like nothing was happening. Now that's a real pro!"

Hank reaches over and wraps an arm around Claire's waist. "Come on, baby, let's dance. I got some new moves I've been meaning to show you."

Claire laughs. "Honey, I saw every move you had a *long* time ago."

"Maybe I'll surprise you tonight," he says playfully.

"I'd die from shock if you got something new to show me, but go ahead and show me anyway, if you think you still can," she purrs.

Hank escorts Claire to the center of the room. There's no dance floor but he pushes back a few empty tables and makes one. They begin to dance check-to-cheek, not noticing, or perhaps caring, Hank's jeans have slipped, exposing the upper regions of his butt crack.

Entry 23: Back again today in the Petrified Forest. Out on Newspaper Rock, above a sandstone outcrop bearing hundreds of petroglyphs—designs scratched out of the rock by ancient artists.

To this day, no one has yet to sort out what the figures and patterns actually mean. I like to think those people created drawings not even they had meanings for just to screw with us centuries later.

Hike out half a mile or so from the small parking lot and

stake out a scenic spot on the edge of a rocky bluff overlooking the natural grasslands. It's sunny and windswept on my high perch, and there's not a soul in sight.

I think: "Now, this is what the road trip is all about! It can't possibly get any better than this!"

I feel a surge of accomplishment that the long road I set out on several months earlier had led me to this very spot. It was never a given I'd actually make it this far, but the fact I did is a real confidence builder for whatever the road ahead may have in store for me.

Brought along my lunch to this high place. Eat baked beans straight from the pintsize pop-top can with a plastic spoon. The cold beans fit right in with the rugged setting. Not so much the bottled sparkling water, almond biscotti, and cup of lemon parfait.

Entry 24: Slip on my protective *snake gaiters* and strike out on foot. As usual, I overestimate my stamina and forget my age, but somehow manage to huff and puff my way around at the fifty-five hundred foot altitude. Even work in some light canyoneering, descents into fissures, as well as equally risky and ill-advised ridge running, which forces me to vault over yawning cracks in the rock formations.

Don't ask me why I do such things. All I know is I can't help myself.

The nonsense doesn't end there.

I really don't know why it's called a Dry Creek Bed*?* It may look that way to the naked eye, but that's no guarantee it is.

Decide to stroll across one such bed paralleling the two-lane road cutting through the vast sweep of sand. An interesting cluster of petrified trees on the far side I want to photograph. I first check out the creek bed, of course. Looks okay. Dry as a bone aside from a few tiny pools of inconsequential water out in the middle. No snakes out sunning. A piece of cake.

The second I step onto the bed I realize I've made a colossal mistake.

The sand gurgles and begins to swallow me, and it's happening fast. I lunge towards the bank I just abandoned, but I'm stuck. I toss my camera back to dry land and then grab hold of the thorny scrub lining the bank. I pull with all my strength. Far too slowly for my liking the sand begins to loosen its death grip and I drag myself out. My jeans are caked in gray-colored muck nearly up to my waist and my hands are bleeding.

A passing Park Ranger spots me standing there in stunned silence and pulls over.

"You okay, sir?" she asks.

"I suppose so," I stammer.

She smiles. "You must promise me you won't be doing this again."

"Oh, I promise. Don't worry about that."

"We'd have one heck of a time finding your body in that goop, if we could find it at all. You'd be stuck there for eternity with whatever else is down below. It would be no fun at all. You realize that, right?"

"Right."

Entry 25: I slowly navigate my way to the valley floor. It's not as easy as I thought it would be. The steep slope is comprised of slippery volcanic ash, topped with a layering of loose pebbles and stones, and millions of tiny, razor-sharp shards of petrified wood.

Takes nearly half an hour of grinding my boots into vague foot holds, and grabbing any rocks and meager vegetation which comes my way, but eventually I make it.

I'm down on the valley floor, dwarfed by gray "elephant skin" clay formations and rolling dunes. Small fossils lay partially exposed here and there, and the site's rich with huge, stunning examples of petrified trees. One appears to still be rooted and there's petrified bark on another. First time I've seen that.

This valley's an exciting find and it's all "mine!" I have a proprietary sense when it comes to certain sites, especially those which require demanding physical exertion on my part to *tame*. I simply want to be left alone to absorb the beauty and character without tourists barging onto *my* turf, especially those toting along protesting children.

When making my way *into* the valley I gave no consideration, of course, to what it will take to get back *out*. Crawl ten feet on my hands and knees, then slide back five. My pant knees shred and dot with blood. Petrified splinters pepper my palms, and volcanic dust assaults my eyes, throat, and nostrils. My big concern is losing footing and tumbling all the way back to the valley floor. Not sure I could muster the strength for another attempt to climb back out. The thought of being stranded there overnight gives me all the incentive I need to redouble my effort to make it on the first try.

As I struggle to save my own hide and the camera strung around my neck, I can't help but notice some kind of large carrion bird eyeballing me from a nearby boulder. I can't be absolutely certain, but it sure looks to me like the bird is salivating.

Entry 26: Decide to stay in the motel room to allow my scrapes, bumps and bruises, and ego, a chance to start healing. That game plan lasts for maybe twenty minutes.

I set out hoping to stumble on a Triassic fossil or two, but settle for a field of petrified trees far out in the golden grasslands. The photographic opportunities are just spectacular. My camera's bulging with at least two hundred shots today alone. Hope to find two or three actual "keepers" out of that. That's pretty close to the typical *success-failure* rate for my photography. Actually, all it really takes is *one* good image to make my day.

On the return leg of the excursion, see that officers have pulled over a white *Ford Mustang* and are going over it from bumper to bumper. Looking for petrified wood, probably. It's illegal to remove it from the park. It's a real problem. Signs everywhere warning it's a crime, but so many people can't resist pocketing a small piece as a souvenir, with the *reasoning* "there's so much of it, it won't be missed." Petrified wood is being carted out park gates at the alarming rate of eight tons a year.

Watching the *The Petrified Forest* as I write this. The old movie popped up on cable tonight. For those of you who haven't seen it, the thirties film features an unhappy, bored waitress, a lost-soul drifter, a killer and his gang, and assorted other characters thrown together one evening at a lonely diner in the Petrified Forest. Made Humphrey Bogart a star.

Bogies best line: *"Since I've been a grownup, I've spent most of my life in prison. I'll probably spend the rest of it dead."*

Entry 27: In the Petrified Forest as evening falls. Taking one last look from the top of Blue Mesa at the setting sun, tonight playing off dramatic black and blue cloud formations which materialized out of seemingly nowhere.

Stay past closing time, somehow managing to avoid detection by park rangers driving around in *S.U.V.'s* rounding up stragglers. My camera's filling fast with images, the most dramatic captured in those special few seconds when day bows to night with one final gasp and *pop* of light.

Blackness cloaks the land and everyone's gone home by the time I reach the South Gate. The U.S. Park Service has obviously anticipated situations like this because the gate opens automatically when I approach it.

I drive on down to the main road, turn right, and head west.

Entry 28: Stop for a hitchhiker. A young kid, maybe twenty, and soaking wet from a passing cloudburst.

Normally I don't stop for hitchhikers. Just too dangerous in these times. But one look at this limp, bedraggled, defeated youngster leaning against a road sign on the highway onramp convinces me he's about at the end of his rope and could really use a break along about now.

He's short, painfully thin, and dressed in jeans, a gray sweatshirt, windbreaker, work boots, and a *Dodgers* baseball cap. His only baggage is a backpack.

"Thanks, mister. Sorry about getting your seat wet."

"Don't worry about it. Where you heading?"

"Sacramento."

"Well, I can probably get you a few hours down the highway."

"Every little bit helps. Much appreciated."

"Sacramento home?"

"Yes, sir. Lived there all my life."

"Going back to see family, huh?"

"Something like that."

We make good time as we roll along through great dry stretches of rocky river valleys sandwiched between treeless hills.

Treat him to lunch at *Burger King*.

Tells me his name is Kenny. Lost his construction job when demand for new housing tanked in California so he headed for Texas to work the oil fields. Had not counted on such stiff competition for jobs in the industry. His lack of actual experience certainly didn't help. To keep his head above water, Kenny took on a series of day labor jobs. Worked a pecan farm for a while. Farmer gave him a tack room in the barn to sleep in. He even managed to last an entire day shoveling manure. Later was hired as a ranch hand, but quickly fired when the owner discovered he couldn't stay on a horse. Slept one night under a tarp in a tool shed behind a garage. Hustled pool from time to time. Washed thousands of dishes.

Checking in back home a few days earlier, his "sometimes" girlfriend told him she was pregnant and wanted to know what he planned to do about it. Kenny did the math and determined he was most likely responsible, so he parked his dreams and headed for Sacramento.

Kenny would have preferred an alternative to marriage, but she was adamant there was only one possible outcome. Kenny knew he was heading down a bad road, but said he felt he had to "do the right thing," even though he didn't like her all that much, or her family.

The kid fully realizes the odds are stacked against him, but he's come up with an outline of a plan he hopes will fly. He'd done roofing before. Lousy work, and he hated it, but it paid okay. He knew "some guys who knew some guys" who owned a roofing company. Maybe they'd take him on "off the books" and part-time, if need be. He could then go to trade school at night and work towards an apprenticeship. Be a plumber, or electrician, maybe. A union job of any kind. That's the ticket.

Kenny drifts off to sleep after lunch, his head resting

against the window. I roll on for another two hours. Let him off at a crossroads town. Slip him a twenty and watch as he enters a pool hall, which also doubles as the bus station.

I turn north at the lone stoplight in town, confident I have another few hours of driving left in me before I'll need to pull over for the night.

Punch the accelerator. The hard afternoon gives way to a softer evening. A low-slung, washed-out moon struggles to be noticed.

Stop for a bite to eat at an old fashioned western saloon which doesn't realize it's retro. Place is practically empty. Strike up an easy conversation with the barmaid-owner. Stay the night.

Entry 29: Not much chance of getting hurt, really hurt, on this road trip. If I can somehow avoid traffic accidents, tornadoes, flash floods, rock slides, quicksand, rattlesnakes, and undercooked chicken wings, I should make out okay.

My background allows me to remain largely under control emotionally when it comes to dealing with challenges out here on the road which could rattle those who've led comparatively sheltered lives...but it doesn't always play out that way. A passing big rig backfired today as I was coming out of a roadside diner. No big deal to everyone but me. Went into a crouch, making myself small, covering my head with my arms. An elderly couple coming out the door behind me asked if I were okay and helped me to my feet. Not exactly a moment to be treasured.

It's pretty clear I still carry around the war years, even after all this time, and they have a bad habit of resurfacing at inconvenient times. Thankfully, I don't cry out in my sleep nearly as much as I once did, and I can usually make it through a violent movie without diverting my eyes. However, I still sit in the back of restaurants and theaters whenever possible, away from the front door. That's where people die when a hand grenade is rolled into the room.

Emotional backlash, and physical wear and tear, is a given for anyone who operates for any extended period of time out on the edge. We field journalists expect it, make allowances for it, adjust the best we can. Problem is there's simply no way to dodge every single *bullet*. Some manage to slip through the defenses. I once went eight months straight without a break of any consequence during one particularly rough patch. Slowed down only when I began to hallucinate. Snakes coiled around my feet and spiders crawling around on my face and in my hair were warning signs something wasn't quite right.

Since we carry no weapons into combat, a journalist's best defense against an especially bad day is to do nothing stupid, if at all possible. Inasmuch as we've seen time and time again how easily and quickly the human body can be rendered useless, we make a point to carefully weigh risks versus rewards before stepping off into the void. Don't get in over our heads, we constantly caution ourselves. Keep in mind no story's worth the sacrifice of life or limb. If we can accomplish that on a regular basis, then chances are we'll get by okay. Then again, there's always the bugaboo which blindsides.

One day back in the early-eighties I'd joined up with a group of reporters trolling the Thai side of the frontier with Cambodia. The Khmer Rouge were engaged in running skirmishes with Vietnamese units in long stretches of border area, causing no end of concern for the Thai military which just wanted to keep the fighting contained inside Cambodia. Not an easy task. The border is ill-defined and the combatants unwilling to respect Thai wishes.

The Thais, short of directly locking horns with the Cambodians or Vietnamese, one afternoon decided to *register* their long guns. That meant firing artillery designed to explode high in the air directly above where the Thais consider the actual border to be, as a clear warning that venturing onto Thai soil would not be tolerated.

We sat in the shade of a towering tree watching the artillery pass overhead, little black specks streaking east. It was an entertaining show until one round registered too close. Way too close. We heard it coming. It sounded different from all the others. A buzzing sound, then a shriek, followed close on by an ear-splitting *crack*.

The round detonated directly above the top of the tree, sending jagged pieces of shrapnel raining down, slapping hard into the ground all around us. One huge piece created a smoldering crater at my feet. If the fifteen-pound chunk of white hot metal had veered slightly to the left, I would have had part, or all, of my head ripped off. Either scenario would have been unacceptable.

I retrieved that shrapnel as a souvenir and still have it today, some thirty years later. I use it as a paperweight.

The granddaddy of all close calls reared its ugly head one morning in Johannesburg when I decided to drive over to the hospital in the South African black township of Alexandra, where street battles had been raging for several days.

I wanted a body count from the hospital staff and to take a look around the grounds, and since the hospital was near the entrance to the township, I calculated I could safely slip in and out, even though anyone with a lick of sense was well-advised to absolutely avoid the area.

The fighting between rival factions of Zulus, one supporting

Nelson Mandela and the other backing Zulu tribal leader Mangosuthu Buthelezi, was ferocious. I could even hear the gunfire from my house a mile or so away as the crow flies, and if the high-altitude African wind was blowing hard in my direction I could make out occasional faint screams. It was not all that uncommon for stray rounds to slice through the trees in my garden, raining down severed leaves and twigs. Once a small bird fell from the sky.

The level of black-on-black violence was at its peak as everyone jockeyed for advantageous position in the so-called *New South Africa*. The country was a powder keg, and the death toll was mounting.

It was reaching the stage where it was actually unsafe to go out on the streets, even in so-called "good" neighborhoods heavily-patrolled by police. I'd been chased several times by car hijackers while commuting between home and my bureau in downtown Johannesburg, where every white person above the age of sixteen seemed to be packing a handgun. A modern day version of the American "Wild West," only one thousand times more dangerous.

Whenever I could pull it off, I went after a human element to my reporting. Not just the dry nuts and bolts numbers on dead and wounded in the endemic violence, but how the violence personally impacted families and communities. And to accomplish that, I had to head to the sound of the suffering.

I talked the security forces into allowing me to ride along in a patrol car on its rounds one Saturday night in Soweto. It was more of a fishing expedition. I didn't have any preconceived notion what would turn up, if anything. I just wanted a better first-hand understanding of the general situation.

The patrol car was actually an armored vehicle, manned by

two burly police officers, both white. The police radio barked constantly once the sun went down. Shootings, grenade explosions, bar fights, rapes, arson, a hacked up body on the side of the road, a suspected "*necklacing.*" That's mob-justice punishment in which a gasoline-filled tire is forced over the victims' shoulders and set alight. It can take a very long time to die.

One call came in for a domestic disturbance. Shots fired and a small explosion of some kind. A number of officers descended on the scene and raced down a narrow, muddy path running between the small, ramshackle tin houses, with me bringing up the rear.

I followed the officers into a house and no sooner than I stepped through the door my feet went out from under me and I toppled to the linoleum floor, landing hard on my ass and finding myself sitting in a slimy substance. The officers hooted and laughed.

"What the hell is this stuff?" I asked, rubbing my sticky hands on the sides of my pants.

"Brains," one snickered. "You're sitting in human brains."

I made one major mistake in attempting to reach the hospital in Alexandra Township. Instead of turning to the right when I drove through the main gate, I went left. I'd been to the hospital before and knew the way, but a momentary lapse in concentration led to the mistake, and in combat zones mistakes are rarely rewarded.

I almost immediately find myself in a residential area of tin and wood shacks, my car surrounded by several hundred young black men with hate-filled eyes, wielding machetes, broad heavy knives called *panga's*, spears, screwdrivers, hammers, clubs and other handy objects guaranteed to cause agonizing death. I can't believe my stupidity.

I quickly calculate I have just two options if there's even the faintest glimmer of hope of getting out of this in one piece. The first is to hit the gas and make a run for it, likely mowing down people in the process, but the probability is high I'll then be dragged from the car and hacked and stomped to death. The second option is to try to bluff my way out of this.

I decide I must do something dramatic, unexpected, and fast, so I leave the "security" of the car, step into the mob, and announce in a loud voice I'm an American journalist, there to do news stories on the terrible situation in the township so the outside world can better understand their plight. It's crucial for them to know right away I'm not one of the hated security forces, but a sympathetic foreigner, hoping that will make a difference.

Inside I'm bleeding, on the outside struggling to maintain a cool, confident demeanor. I instinctively know if I show any fear, any fear at all, I will die right then and there. I'm guided by the *logic* that a pride of lions is more likely to attack a lame water buffalo trying to flee than a healthy one standing its ground, or something along those lines.

The crowd moves in tight. They're right in my face. The young men are mumbling to one another in Zulu, clearly discussing what to do with me, maybe even debating which one of them will get *kill rights*.

My biggest fear in those early seconds is someone will succumb to the overwhelming temptation to take me down. All it would take is one thrust of a knife and it would be over.

One man not ten feet away waves a machete over his head and begins chanting and bobbing up and down, bare feet slapping the ground. I don't know what it all means, but suspect it's not good. I want to cry out for my mother, but will not give them the satisfaction. Resolutely standing my ground will be my last act of defiance, the one I carry to the grave with me. I tell myself to give them nothing to gloat over later as they recount details of my death. Okay, maybe I'll gasp when the blade cuts, but I'm determined to let the life flow out of me in silence, even if the pain is unbearable. I was angry now, angry as I've ever been. Angry at myself for such stupidity, angry at these people who held my life in their hands, angry at *God* for making us all so imperfect.

Then a voice. An angelic voice. Almost surreal. A petite, young black woman in a nurse's uniform pushes her way through the crowd and speaks to me loudly so all can hear.

"Can you please drive me to the hospital? It's not far and I would be most grateful."

I'm the grateful one. A ray of hope. Maybe not much, but at least something.

She slides into the car and frantically motions for me to follow. I slip back behind the wheel, far from confident I'll be allowed to leave, but will know the answer to that soon enough. I start the car and slowly move forward. The crowd parts.

We head down the dirt road. I feel groggy, sick to my stomach. My hands are shaking. I'm sure I soiled myself.

The nurse looks at me disapprovingly and shakes her head. "I could not believe what I saw there. You, man, are very brave, or very stupid."

My voice is a whisper. "I'm not brave."

Entry 30: I make my way there on a straight, two-lane road cutting through a colorless stretch of the Painted Desert, but eventually find myself on a winding road framed by rolling hills rich with wild flowers.

I soon reach my destination, Fort Apache.

From its founding in the heart of Apache Country in

eighteen seventy, until Geronimo's capture sixteen years later, the cavalry of Fort Apache was regularly locked in skirmishes with various Apache renegade bands.

Not much remains of the fort. A boarding school's there now, but surviving bits and pieces of the old fort are scattered about. The first commanding officer's cabin remains, along with several barracks. The stockade and commissary storehouse have all but collapsed. There's an operating post office. Area code's 85926, by the way. Stumbled on a hilltop cemetery at the end of a dirt road, the final resting place for soldiers, civilians and Indian Scouts alike. It's choked with weeds and appears to have been all but forgotten.

I appreciate the still largely untamed nature of much of these tribal lands where so much history and myth unfolded, including five centuries of Apache presence in the area, and there appears to be no attempt to capitalize on the famous name of the fort. There's a small museum on site, but no nearby hotels, casinos, restaurant chains, and cheesy gift shops which, in my view, desecrate so many historical sites in these parts.

Fort Apache. A nice find.

Entry 31: Winslow, Arizona. Standing on a corner looking for a girl in a flatbed *Ford*, one slowing down to take a look at me. But there's no girl, no one to lighten my load, to take me in. I guess she had a flat tire.

Entry 32: I've lost count of the number of times friends, and even strangers I meet out on the road, ask me if I'm not lonely flitting from place to place, week after week, month after month, with only myself for company most of the time.

My stock answer is there's a great deal of difference between being lonely and being alone. Some people understand that, others are unable to differentiate between the two.

Highway miles are long miles. For some, desolate miles. Not everyone's suited to the challenge of solitary travel and require the constant wrap of people to feel whole and valued. Not me. I require solitude as much as I need air, food, water, and light.

Entry 33: Stop off for lunch in yet another dreary desert town. Restaurant's a stand-alone, single-story, white-washed building in the middle of a quarter-acre asphalt parking lot.

Old school vinyl booths, worn linoleum floor curling at the corners. In need of a paint job. A totally out-of-place Parisian mural stretches nearly the entire length of one wall. Cashier's doing her nails while talking on the phone. Big portions of Mexican-American food served up at a reasonable price. Mostly Native American and Hispanic clientele. People know one another. Lots of cross-chatter between tables and booths.

The restaurant sits alongside an especially bleak stretch of *Route 66* which slices through the center of town and once served as its primary economic engine. No more. There's a closed gas station across the street from the restaurant, its gas pumps ripped from the foundation, windows covered in large sheets of plywood. The surviving *Texaco* sign still looms overhead, recalling the day when a gallon of gasoline cost forty-one cents.

A few doors up the street is the *Desert Motel.* Metal sign above the lobby entrance reads "Open for Business," but the place is gutted. Big pile of rusted air conditioners off to one side. Weeds growing through cracks in the pavement.

Not many tourists venture off the nearby interstate these days and most of the shops in the downtown area are vacant with "For Rent" signs taped to the windows. But the restaurant, according to the large sign on the street-side wall of the building, boasts it's been in the same family since nineteen forty-nine, somehow managing to buck the trend and hang on.

For those who argue Americans are spoiled, greedy, and have too much "stuff," they've never seen this town, or the scores of others like it out on the far, mostly forgotten fringes of this land. Grit, pride, and a fiercely independent streak are about all many of these people have left going for them, and while that may not be enough to ensure long-term survival, it's at least something.

Sitting in a booth waiting for my order of tacos and re-fried beans, sipping on a huge, sweating red plastic glass of ice tea, I look through the half-open window blinds and across the sun-savaged parking lot where I spot an old man in a cowboy hat sitting on a walker a few feet from the road. Just calmly sitting there, watching the cars pass by.

I motion for the waitress to come over and point at the old man. "He's kind of close to the road, isn't he?"

The name tag on her light blue uniform lets me know her name is Beverly. She's in her forties. One of those people with a perpetually sunny disposition. Her dyed bright red hair is tucked up under a hair net and her makeup is several applications too thick.

"Oh, that's Morgan!" she announces in a strong voice, causing everyone in the restaurant to look out the row of windows. "An Indian elder, or something like that."

"Yep, that's Morgan, alright," a Native American man in the booth three down from mine tells everyone what they already know.

Another man at the far end of the restaurant shouts to Beverly. "He still ordering chocolate milk every meal?"

"You betcha! "

This triggers a ripple of laughter. I sense it would be next to impossible to maintain a sense of privacy in a town this small.

The waitress tells me the old man leaves home every single morning around eleven and plants himself in his walker alongside *66,* and patiently waits for anyone who happens to be passing, friend or stranger, to stop and offer him a ride. He then reverses the process after his meal.

"It's a nice sunny day," Beverly notes. "There are days when the weather's not so great, but Morgan always seems to find a way to make it here anyway. Sometimes he gets a ride right away, other times it can take a while. If he's still sitting out there when I finish my shift at three, I drive him home. Sometimes I have him over for dinner. He and my daddy and old man talk hunting and stuff for hours. Poor guy lives all alone. Wife died some time back and his daughter moved to Oregon last year when her husband got a job in a brewery out there."

The man is still sitting there, not two feet off *66*, when I leave the restaurant. I pull up alongside and lean out the window. "Need a lift? Beverly says you might."

His response is deadpan. "She's a nice lady. Just wish she'd do something about her mustache."

This guy is okay.

I fold his walker and store it in the backseat of the *Mazda* and we head west down Main Street. He asks that instead of being taken home I drive him to the *Walmart* sitting on top of the interstate on the far side of town. "I haven't aggravated them in a while," he grins.

Morgan's dressed in a buffalo *Stetson* pulled low over a full head of white hair, dark blue slacks, a faded orange *Polo* shirt, a leather vest decorated with blue beads, and scuffed cowhide boots. His face is weatherworn, the color bearing a striking similarity to the dominant shade of earth in the surrounding Painted Desert his people call home. Says his tribal name is *Big Boy*, but Morgan will do.

He's eighty-one. His back is bent, legs in full rebellion. His hands resemble the surface roots of old trees.

We drive no more than a few blocks when Morgan begins to grimace. He's clearly in pain.

"You okay?" I ask.

"Not for a long time." His voice is now gravelly and shallow.

"Want some *Aleve*? I have a bottle in the glove compartment."

"No, thank you. I have some pain killers at home. Just forget to bring them along when I set out this morning, not that they do me much good anymore."

Morgan began life on the nearby tribal reservation. As a boy, he developed a love for the land, the wildlife, and the rodeo. Joined the Air Force when the Korean War broke out. Shattered his left leg "and pretty much the whole side of my body when my plane was shot up and we were forced to crash land our bomber." Morgan is taking quick, shallow breaths as he runs his hand along his left side ribcage, the memory of that day those many decades ago written all over his face.

Morgan tells me he recovered from his war wounds and joined the rodeo, of all things. Competed for years, "from Texas to Canada, and back again. Won lots, too...I was young and strong. Could take just about anything thrown at me on the circuit. Couldn't do nothing, though, about the passage of time." So Morgan retired and returned home to be near the tribal lands he walked as a boy.

We're driving through a concrete jungle of motels, fast food restaurants, gas stations and convenience stores which had mushroomed all along the busy *Interstate Corridor.*

"This all was once farmland not so long ago, and before that it was *our* land," Morgan says without rancor. It's just a statement of fact.

"Life has changed so much," he adds. "Everyone moves now. Always moving. Never stopping to look or listen. Such restless spirits. Not like before."

His voice trails off to a near whisper. "I think I've lived too long."

Entry 34: The humble sandwich is easily one of the greatest inventions of all-time. Not quite up there, maybe, with the wheel, printing press, telephone, breast implants, and internal combustion engine, but it certainly ranks well above the movie rating system, dry cleaning, the electric guitar, grocery store coupons, and *AstroTurf.*

It's perfect! Nourishing, simple, compact, mobile, versatile, and inexpensive. The ideal road companion. I might have succumbed to malnutrition on this trip by now had I not been able to pull one at will from the mini beverage cooler I keep on the seat beside me on those long stretches of open road with few culinary options worth exploring, or none at all.

I usually try to slap together a few sandwiches each morning in my motel room, place them in zip-lock bags, and then into the cooler, along with any ice I can lay my hands on. Mayonnaise and desert heat do not mix well, so keeping most things chilled is imperative.

My favorite sandwich is easily the venerable peanut butter and jelly. I simply won't consider traveling without a jar or two of peanut butter. It doesn't require refrigeration, is rich in protein, and can be eaten straight from the jar, with my fingers if necessary. Actually tastes better that way.

Entry 35: The older I get, the earlier I rise, although climbing out of bed before the rooster crows has left me neither healthy, nor wealthy, nor even wise, it has allowed me the pleasure to stand witness to the dawn of each new day. To me, the still beauty of the break of day is nature's gift to us. It's *her* way of reassuring us everything's going to be alright.

There are mornings on this road trip as the early light gathers itself, something quite unexpected happens. My camera pushes me aside and takes on a life of its own, conspiring with nature and becoming a veritable paintbrush. I'd like to take credit for the end result, but I know it would be a lie.

Entry 36: Southwestern Utah. Dawn. At high altitude. Nine thousand feet. The external temperature reading on the trip computer says it's twenty-eight. That can't be. I pullover and step from the car. Feels even colder. Retrieve a sweatshirt and windbreaker from the rear of the *Mazda*.

Some place I find myself—raw, rugged and unapologetic. Feel I'm stranded at the far outer edge of the world, and then some, and not another person's around to help me ward off the sense of dread.

The serpentine road is buffeted by gales slicing through the pink and orange canyons. Great rock formations hover over and around me. I run a gauntlet of sandstone pillars, slickrock domes, palisade walls, flatrocks rich with needles and spires, and mazes of side canyons anchored by great stone arches. This badland sculpted by time is alive with ghostly shadows dancing between the rocks and howling shrieks carried on the tireless wind.

I swallow hard and head north, deeper into the waiting desolation.

Entry 37: Giant sloths once walked this land. Mammoth and camel, too. They're gone now, of course, along with the people who hunted them thousands of years ago, but the rugged landscape remains the same. It takes a good million years for the elements to put even a minor dent in the geological layout. What the ancients saw back then is exactly what I'm looking at today, and what our descendants will encounter thousands of years from now.

I've never seen anything quite like this place and it grows more visually intriguing as the cliff-hugging switchback road takes me ever deeper into this meeting point of the Colorado Plateau and Great Basin. Towering sandstone cliffs and tilting, vast monolithic towers of red, pink, yellow and beige lord over me. Ponderosa pine and juniper sprout from narrow crevices in the rock, roots digging into the joints and fissures in search of precious water, splitting rock as they travel. They remind me of Japanese *bonsai* with their twisted shapes and artistically pruned appearance. Below, cottonwoods spread their sheltering limbs over the banks of the slow-moving Virgin River, a blue-green ribbon meandering along the valley floor. It's the source of life for cattails, willows and rushes, and hanging gardens of fern, wildflowers and mosses...for the mule deer and canyon tree frogs, the mountain lion, ringtail cat, whiptail lizard, beaver, tortoise, and bighorn sheep. Valley breezes and updrafts ferry willow flycatchers, yellow warblers, swifts, and leathery pipistrelles up to the pygmy woodlands, and beyond to the slot canyons and plateau mixed conifer forests of Douglas fir, white pine, and aspen.

Entry 38: Stop for a late lunch at *The Buffalo Trails Trading Company*. Have the place all to myself. Italian opera's blaring out over the sound system when you'd expect something *twangy*. Slip into a booth and order a buffalo burger with all the trimmings.

The guy who does the cooking and manages the adjoining gift shop tells me the meat comes from a herd raised on a ranch about an hour or so to the north. Lectures me on the health benefits of buffalo meat. Low in fat, easier to digest. Goes on to say *The Disney Channel's* contracted to rent out the place for six days to film the ending of a made-for-cable movie.

The restaurant's located on a flat stretch of road near the town of Virgin, population two hundred seventy-four, according to the welcoming sign. Virgin made national headlines some years back when the town, fearing its Second Amendment right to bear arms was under fire, enacted an ordinance requiring a gun and ammunition in every home for residents' self-defense. Failure to pack *heat* in Virgin gets you a stiff fine.

The ordinance caught the eye of Michael Moore, the gadfly of all things corporate, who brought his cameras to Virgin to film a segment of *Bowling for Columbine*, which tackled America's relationship with firearms. Won an *Oscar*.

Not to be outdone by tiny Virgin, neighboring La Verkin passed an ordinance declaring the town of thirty-five hundred a "United Nations-free zone," whatever that is.

Everywhere I go out here people seem so angry, threatened, frustrated, and put upon. They see the land they love slipping away and being absorbed by a world they no longer understand and have a say in. If there's ever a new armed revolution in the country it could very well begin right here. The first shoots of the seeds of discontent are already breaking through the soil and the roots are fast-spreading. This place bears watching.

Entry 39: Saw an accident today. A minivan left the road and slammed into a guardrail above a deep ravine, did a one eighty and then hit the guardrail again. The van was pretty well chewed up.

I pull over, of course, and race to the vehicle, along with a dozen other eyewitnesses. Inside are three young children and a woman I assume is their mother. All the children are girls. One child, the youngest, is cut by flying glass. The mother is semi-conscious and mumbling incoherently. The other two girls, around seven and eight, are crying but appear unhurt. I take turns applying pressure to a gash on the girls' right arm. She doesn't say a word. Just looks straight ahead. Shock, I suspect.

The uninjured girls are pulled from the wreckage and being comforted on a grassy slope a short distance away. A woman applies a damp cloth to the forehead of the mother who's still behind the wheel, but has yet to fully come around.

Some raw emotion on display by the responders. No breast-beating, but just enough of a reaction to do a possible disservice to the already terrified children. I debate suggesting they rein it in a notch, but decide not to risk aggravating the situation.

While my exposure to torn flesh over the years largely inured me to rather "commonplace" mishaps, allowing me to take care of most business without undue fanfare, it wasn't always like that. Back at the beginning of my career, I'd often find myself teetering on the edge of an emotional meltdown by the horror I saw inflicted on the most helpless of us, especially children.

The worst of it for me was in Cambodia. Those memories are pretty much as vivid today as they were so long ago when I was living the nightmare. Oh, I've tried to file away that part of my life, but memories have a bad habit of infiltrating my defenses and making it tough on me from time to time.

It all dated back to Christmas, nineteen seventy-eight. I'd just arrived in Bangkok to run the news bureau there when Vietnam invaded neighboring Cambodia and quickly ousted the ruling Khmer Rouge, triggering a human stampede west in the direction of the frontier with Thailand. Not only was the heavily-armed Khmer Rouge in full flight, but several million civilians as well who'd been living under the heavy hand of the communists for the past four years.

The bloodletting during that period had been ferocious as the Khmer Rouge, under a madman and no-quarter ideologue named Pol Pot, systematically murdered at will under a genocidal purification policy designed at eliminating the educated class and creating a feudal, agrarian society...a land with no schools, books, independent thinking, families, even love. These fuckers made the Taliban look like pikers.

As many as four million innocents had already died in the horror that was Cambodia, and there was more to come. Only this time I was there to see it.

Despite the fact the Khmer Rouge had been routed by the Vietnamese, they still had a vice-like grip on most of the refugee population, and used the hastily-erected, primitive border encampments as launching pads to strike against the Vietnamese who were active in the area. Blood flowed freely.

The refugee flight to the border with Thailand began as a trickle, but quickly escalated into a tidal wave of the walking dead, with every imaginable physical and emotional horror on full display.

The numbers fleeing Cambodia swelled onto the hundreds of thousands, then one million, then two. No exact head counts were possible in that grisly march of tortured, decimated bodies limping through seas of tall grass and down narrow mountain paths cutting through the thick jungle.

Forward they came, a silent procession of brutalized men, women and children, sapped of strength, some missing limbs and hobbling along on crutches, people bent low and sagging under the weight of their few remaining worldly possessions strapped to their backs.

Most of the human wreckage was starving, surviving on roots and leaves, and bark stripped from trees. So many were injured and wounded, and stricken with the many strains of malaria, dysentery, and other pestilence borne of the years of neglect. The threat of bubonic plague was very real.

This ancient civilization hovered precariously on the brink of extinction, and it was touch-and-go for the next year or so.

The Border, as we fifty or so members of the Bangkok-based foreign press corps came to call it, seized control of our lives. We'd caravan over many mornings, a two-hour drive from Bangkok, and then disperse to look for news stories, of which there was no shortage.

Days become weeks, weeks became months, then time pretty much lost all meaning. Journalists covering the story in the fetid refugee camps and across the battle-scarred landscape recycled the misery over and over again in a blizzard of news copy and photographs which brought the plight of these suffering people to world attention. It was exhausting, emotionally-draining work.

From time to time I'd break away from the journalistic herd and strike out on my own into some of the more remote areas of the countryside in an attempt to reconnect with myself, brush aside the mental cobwebs, and summon up those inner resources I knew I'd require for the challenges ahead.

One day finds me well off the beaten path, in a section of the frontier I'd yet to explore.

I'm driving through a region of rice paddies, orchards, fields of grazing buffalo, and tiny villages where time passes effortlessly and uneventfully, as it has since before recorded time. I reach a dusty crossroads a few miles from Cambodia, or at least where I think Cambodia should be. No road signs pointing the way. I turn left. I'm pretty sure that's east. The sun's directly overhead so I have trouble telling with absolute certainty which way is which. I remind myself I really do need to start carrying around a compass.

I drive maybe one mile down a dirt road with no name, in a place with no name, when I spot something off to the right. A human shape, maybe. Something. I stop to investigate, going against my better judgment, always a risky proposition in a place where *AK-47's* outnumber people with common sense. If I were a little older and a lot wiser, I would probably keep going, but curiosity takes command.

I walk just a few yards off the road when I come upon the scene.

A semi-conscious woman lies in a mud wallow her writhing body dug out of the earth at the edge of a slimy, mosquito-infested pond.

She's young. Around twenty. Dressed in a filthy white t-shirt and a threadbare *sampot*, a likely remnant from a life long ago, in a far happier time.

She's curled in a fetal position, hands tightly pressed against her temples, face frozen in unimaginable pain. I suspect cerebral malaria. I've seen it in the camps. Brutal, cruel, and deadly, even with decent medical care.

She apparently senses my presence and begins to whimper. She rolls over and looks at me through half-mast eyelids.

It's then I see she's lying in a shallow pool of bloody dysentery which has soaked through her clothing.

The horror escalates. Over my left shoulder a sound, and close. I turn. Not ten feet away, in a puddle of water, sits a little boy, stark naked. I guess his age at around eighteen months. He's oblivious to the world around him, and his sore-covered, sunburned body bears the earmarks of advancing starvation: orange hair, stick limbs, sunken cheeks, saucer-eyes, distended stomach...

I immediately turn my attention to the toddler, who appears to be the most salvageable of the pair. He feels like a sack of feathers in my arms as I carry him back to the car, an old station wagon which has seen better days, but is proving to be a reliable and sturdy form of transportation on these harsh, backcountry roads.

I carry two five-gallon tins of water in the rear of the wagon along with assorted towels and cloths, and a totally useless medical kit. I'll need more than iodine and *Band-Aids* to deal with this mess.

I lay the child on the backseat, dampen a washcloth and began to carefully wash away some of the caked mud from his face, hands, and scalp. I stop when I see his hair's falling out in clumps. I try to give the boy a sip of water I've poured onto a spoon, but he jerks his head away. I then soak a fresh hand towel in water and place it near his mouth, just touching his cracked lips. Nursing instincts take hold and he eagerly sucks on the piece of cloth. I return to the mother.

I carry her a few yards to a cluster of banyan trees with the intention of making a bed of some sort for her in the rear compartment of the wagon, but first I want to get her out of the sun and that bloody fecal pool. Maybe get some water into her.

She's trembling now, gasping for breath. Body's on fire. I

pour water on her neck and sprinkle a little on her face. I'm sure it doesn't help in the slightest, but I have to make do with what little I have. Besides, I'm no doctor. What the hell do I know?!

I try to formulate a plan. Maybe there's a clinic in one of the villages I passed through on the way here. I'll try that first, but if I come up blank I'll push on to one of the camps where international relief workers have set up tent hospitals. That's her best and last hope, and chance for her child to pull through.

When I turn my gaze back to the woman, she's gone.

Died holding my hand.

She gave no wail, whimper, or gasp at the last. Just died.

I'm struck by how serene her face is now. The agony's been swept away. She's somewhere else. All that's left behind of what she had been is a collection of bones in a shattered casing, unburdened of a short, unspeakable life which offered precious little over which to rejoice.

I brush away the hair from her face and battle the urge to erupt, but I simply don't have time to waste right now on an emotional outburst. Maybe later.

There's a child to be saved, but I must move quickly...

Entry 40: The old fashioned road map has fallen on hard times. Better highway signage and inventions like Ground Positioning Satellite no longer make it necessary for a traveler to spread out a cumbersome paper map across the expanse of dashboard, and then try to figure out where all those eye-straining, crisscrossing, multicolored, vein-like lines are heading before a journey can begin with any degree of confidence they'll be a successful outcome to a long day on the road.

Oh, those maps are still around. I know because I collect them. My glove compartment and seatback pockets are stuffed with them.

Each state issues its own map. They're usually called something along the lines of *Official Transportation Guide*, and are a virtual encyclopedia of travel. There's a full-size map of the entire state, of course, along with small, detailed maps of the major population centers. There are charts and other devices to help the traveler locate individual towns, along with driving distances and times, where to find state and national parks, toll roads, and Amtrak stations. There's also emergency contact information, special traffic regulations and various road classifications unique to the state. The maps often include a welcome from the governor, telling you how much the state appreciates your visit and just how confident everyone is you'll have the time of your life.

These maps are available immediately after you enter most states, at so-called *Welcome Centers*, well-manicured sanctuaries just off the highway, offering bathrooms, vending machines, picnic tables, and dog walk areas.

To get your hands on an actual road map you must sometimes deal with a state employee sitting behind a counter dispensing travel information and advice.

As often as not, that person is an elderly woman bearing a striking physical resemblance to my home room teacher in high school. Not such a good thing.

No question Miss Best hated my guts but, looking back, I really can't fault her. Poor woman surely had her fill of slovenly, unmotivated, obnoxious students in the half century she'd been teaching, and the sight of me slumped over my desk a few feet away from her during the first period of each school day must have been unbearable. I'd like to locate Miss Best and apologize to her, but she'd be at least one hundred twenty-five years-old by now.

Anyway, there was a time when you could snap up a road

map and be on your merry way without dealing with *your own Miss Best*. That's usually no longer the case. First, you may have to answer a series of questions put to you. "*Where are you from?" "How long will you be visiting our fair state?" "Is this your first visit?"*

My all-time favorite*: "How did you hear about our state?"*

"Probably in third grade," I mumbled.

The *Welcome Center* is also a good place to pick up one of those motel discount coupon books. I've shaved *big* money from my road trip using them, an important consideration given I'm struggling to stay within budget as gas prices soar. It's reached the point I pretty much won't stay in a motel if I'm unable to present a discount coupon, unless it's late at night, and I have little choice.

It's during *these* times I've been known to haggle over price, a habit acquired in markets and shops around the world, but an art form seldom seen on the American landscape outside of car dealerships and Christmas tree lots. A quoted room rate of fifty dollars is countered with thirty. Sometimes the desk clerk simply rejects the offer and I can either pay the asking price or be on my way. Usually pride and stubbornness makes me choose the latter, even though I'm exhausted and need a room in the worst way.

Then there are times the bargaining is fast and furious, and the final room rate can be cut by one-third, or even more. The haggling process is made easier by the fact so many entry-level motels and low-end chain franchises these days are owned and operated by foreign nationals from lands where vigorous price negotiation is an integral part of the culture.

Snug in my hopefully deeply-discounted room, I often find myself pouring over newly-acquired road maps in bed each evening, on the look-out for obscure little gems which may have otherwise eluded my eye. Places like the *Mojave Museum of History and Arts,* where the movie career of hometown hero Andy Devine is celebrated. Groom, Texas, proved to be an absolute gold mine. Not only will you find the largest cross in the Western Hemisphere, nineteen stories high, but nearby is the still standing leaning water tower, which awed travelers for decades along *Route 66.*

For such a compact-looking item, when unfolded a map covers a lot of real estate. Getting the map back into its original shape is another matter entirely. The two dozen or more folds so neat, crisp and precise coming from the printer, become lumpy and misshapen after I get my hands on them, and they're never the same after that, even if I sit on them, sandwich them between books, or go on the attack with a steam iron.

While the old paper map holds a sentimental place in my heart, I increasingly find myself relying on the Global Positioning System to navigate my way cross-country. At first, I treated GPS as a novel gadget, interesting but ultimately of little value. Just one of those new electronic toys my bevy of grandkids and their parents are so fond of but, in my antiquated view, deprived us of our ability to think, to reason, to navigate by instinct. But the GPS is *now* an indispensable companion. Methodically, without emotion, it guides me out of tight jams late at night when hemmed in by deepening darkness, the heavens unloading a torrent of rain, or blizzard of sand.

I hate admitting this, but I actually find myself talking to the GPS voice built into my phone, a *woman* with a no nonsense disposition.

"We getting close to the destination, Mildred?" I call her Mildred. "Any word on traffic conditions ahead?" "About time for lunch, don't you think?"

She never answers me directly. Only talks when she wants to, and then only to boss me around.

I sure wish my GPS companion had at least a hint of a personality instead of that sterile, robotic voice. It would be a nice feature as I hit the road each day for her to wish me a simple "good morning," or perhaps even compliment me on how dapper I look on those rare occasions when I wear a fresh shirt and my hair is actually combed.

A little acerbic wifely manner would even be welcome as a change of pace from time to time when I unforgivingly fail to properly heed driving instructions being dispensed.

"Are you deaf?! I said turn right, not left! You're a hopeless case! You never pay attention to me when I speak! I should have listened to my mother and married Marvin Greenberg!"

Entry 41:

Humankind has not woven the web of life.
We are but one thread within it.
Whatever we do to the web, we do to ourselves.
All things are bound together.
All things connect.

~Native American, ca. 1850

I move cautiously along a narrow ledge wrapping around a hill so I can get a better view of the valley floor below.

One false step and I'll plunge several hundred feet to a bed of boulders. Venturing from the most worn of paths is discouraged around here, but this is the *only* way I can escape all those tourists clucking and clicking around me.

Rounding a corner I see him sitting there on the ground leaning back against a sheer rock wall, gazing out at the vastness. It's a middle-age Native American man with a profile identical to the image on the Indian Head Nickel. His hair is long and he's dressed in a plain white shirt and jeans, but is shoeless. His skin's the color of a ruby.

He's chanting in a near whisper and holding a snow white eagle feather in his right hand, which he extends at arm's length towards an eagle gliding high above on a thermal.

He drops his arm to his side when he sees me. I startled him but he quickly recovers and smiles warmly. "Welcome! Come, sit," he says, patting the ground beside him.

When I hesitate, he slaps the ground twice. "Come, friend. There are no strangers here and there is more than enough for one man."

I feel as if I'm intruding on something solemn and private, but take a seat beside him on the rock hard earth.

The land below is spread out like an orange blanket across a flat plain from which sprout widely-spaced buttes, mesas, and free-standing monoliths, all aglow and casting long shadows in the late-afternoon sun.

This is Monument Valley.

Since I was a boy watching John Wayne in all those John Ford westerns set in this very valley, I've dreamed of the day when I, too, could walk this land.

We're silent this man and I, absorbed by the panorama nature is gifting us. I eventually whisper how beautiful it all is. The man agrees it is indeed a fine sight.

I feel all stress drain from my body and drift off to sleep. When I open my eyes, the light of day is in full retreat. The man is gone, but in my lap is a feather from an eagle.

Entry 42: It's rare these days to find undisturbed places as nature created them. Such is the hand of *man*.

At least the American people had the good sense to realize long ago what remained of our unique national heritage would soon vanish forever without strong-willed, concrete action. From that moment of sanity emerged our national parks, an idea which has been nurtured and improved upon by each succeeding generation.

Not only do these vast expanses of virgin land allow us a pure glimpse into our world as it was thousands of years ago, but it's in these parks we can find a deeper connection to ourselves, a place for spiritual balance, refuge from a troubled world.

Entry 43: Wanted to write something here about the futility and folly of war. Heard on the evening news four NATO troops had died in Afghanistan. Roadside bomb. Just can't get into all that right now, however. Feeling lousy. Headache, groggy, exhausted, no appetite. Gasping for air today after climbing a modest hill for an unencumbered view of a deep canyon. Likely a case of altitude sickness. Had been warned to be on the alert for it. Can be deadly. Will take it extra easy the rest of the evening and seek out a somewhat lower altitude in the morning if I'm not feeling better by then.

Entry 44: Going no place in particular. Just drifting about taking in the scenery when a road sign alerts me I can find the Navajo Nation if I take the next exit off the highway.

I decide to take a look. I know from experience by now I'll be in for a long drive through unforgiving land along suspect roads, but there's no longer anything new in that.

I head north, cutting through an arid, barren land of blue-tinged cliffs and canyons, prominent features in the southern reaches of the Black Mesa, on the Colorado Plateau.

Sun's beating down hard. No towns, rest stops, gas stations. A lousy place to have car trouble. *Mazda's* purring, thankfully. I have the feeling the little car actually enjoys these challenges. One of these days I'll splurge and fill her up with a tank of *high-octane* gasoline as a reward for services rendered.

An hour or so later, I emerge from the depths of the badlands into a grazing landscape spread out all the way to the distant curvature of the earth. This is the true heart of Navajo Country, the seat of government of the largest sovereign Native American nation in North America.

A road sign along the way informs me matter-of-factly the laws of the United States carry little weight here and I will be subject to Navajo justice should I do anything to displease the tribe. I decide, of course, to be on my best behavior, but don't have a clue what constitutes violations of their laws and culture. I'll just have to wing it and hope for the best.

A lot of blood and tears were shed on this very land. The invading cavalry responded to Navajo raids in the area by forcing thousands of starving tribes' people on the infamous *Long Walk,* and internment in a faraway place. I seem to recall Kit Carson played a major role in that travesty, just one of scores inflicted on the Native American tribes out here which pretty much just wanted to be left in peace.

I pull over at what a small, hand-painted sign describes as a *Picnic Area.* Need to stretch my legs, take a leak, maybe eat something.

Not much to this wayside out in the middle of nowhere. A small dirt clearing in a cluster of stunted trees a few feet off the road. There's a picnic table caked in bird shit and a dented metal trash can chained to a wooden stake. Not sure I want to eat anything in this place, but I suppose a piss would be okay.

No sooner than I step from the car I see them, but certainly not before they saw me. Two medium size dogs, golden in color and achingly thin, staring at me with flat yellow eyes. I can't get a read if they're hostile or merely curious, or simply waiting for a handout from a passing tourist, which is possibly how they survive in this wilderness.

I'm moved by their pitiful condition so decide to do something about it. I don't have much with me. An orange won't cut it, but maybe they'll be happy with granola bars. I retrieve several from the car, unwrap one and hold it out in front of me. One dog immediately backs away, but the other, after some thought, slowly approaches one cautious half step at a time, eyes locked on the food. When he cuts the distance between us to a few feet he snatches the bar from my hand and inhales it, never bothering to chew. Reminds me of my roommate my freshman year in college. The dog then moves maybe ten feet away, sits and just stares at me. A blank stare. No show of emotion of any kind.

The other animal has retreated behind the trash can, but hunger compels him to approach me, two steps forward, and one step back. Then, in one seamless moment, everything changes. A transformation...from timorous to rapacious. A coarse utterance bubbles up from a place primal. Eyes flip from wary to dark and cold. Head drops between hunched shoulders. Hind quarters tremble, a prelude to a lunge. On my left flank, a few yards away, the confederate joins the flourish of fangs, and is slowly moving in on me, surrendering to ancient imperatives.

Being quick on the uptake, I realize my kindness this morning will unlikely be reciprocated, so I drop the granola bar and hightail it to the car, fully expecting to lose a chunk of my ass as I flee. When I look back from the safety of the car interior, the animals have vanished.

A few miles down the road it dawns on me what I'd done,

and I'm not pleased. I'd not hand-fed stray dogs, as I thought, but a pair of coyotes, likely driven by hunger to interact with humans. I'm dumbfounded by my stupidity. Another one of those momentary mental lapses I can ill afford. I count my fingers and am somewhat surprised to find they're all still attached to my hands.

It's high noon when I reach a town. A bump in the vastness. Dusty and dry. Not much in the way of vegetation. Horses, pigs, and chickens running free in the streets. The houses and buildings are uninspired, old and neglected.

But there's a *McDonald's*! There's *always* a *McDonald's,* it seems. Spot the *Golden Arch* rising above a row of shacks.

Drop by for fries and a vanilla shake. The familiar food gives me the illusion I'm still on planet earth. Take some comfort in that.

Place is packed with the lunch crowd and I'm the sole non-Native American there. Navajo and Hopi patrons only, as far as I can tell.

The Navajo are heavyset and robust, dressed pretty much as I am, and easy to talk to. The Hopi, on the other hand, are aloof and buttoned-up, at least when I'm around.

Try striking up conversations with Hopi at nearby tables, but get nowhere. Just grunts and averted eyes. I have a feeling they don't like outsiders very much which, in my estimation, shows uncommon good sense.

Nobel looking people these Hopi. Short, muscular, high cheek bones, slanting eyes, dark-skinned. Some of the men have banged or terraced hair, the older women sport something approximating pigtails, and I spot a young girl wearing her hair in a whorl on the side of her head. Reminds me of Princess Leia in *Star Wars.*

I'm struck by the fact so many of the Hopi are going about their day in traditional dress, or some variation of it, far more so than other tribes I've run across out here in the Southwest, which seem more inclined to blending in.

The Hopi Reservation is completely surrounded by the far larger Navajo Nation, and I hear trouble bubbles up now and then between the tribes. Thousand year-old disputes die hard in this hard land where survival is never a given, even now.

Times like this make me feel I've been propelled back a century or more in time to when William Henry Jackson and Frank Reinhart took their cameras out among the Native American tribes and captured all those enduring iconic images. Some of the likeliness's of those images are possible to photograph out here even today, if you look hard enough and don't get in people's faces. A telephoto lens is a good way to avoid dustups with camera-shy locals.

Entry 45: Came across this century and a half old quote from a disheartened and dismayed Native American chieftain as he stood witness to his ancient civilization crumbling under the heavy boot of the white man sweeping across the land like a swarm of locusts, devouring everything in its path:

"How can you buy or sell the sky, the warmth of the land? The idea is strange to us. If we do not own the freshness of the air and the sparkle of the water, how can you buy them? Every part of this earth is sacred to my people. Every shining pine needle, every sandy shore, every mist in the dark woods, every clearing and humming insect is holy in the memory and experience of my people. The sap which courses through the trees carries the memories of the red man. The white man's dead forget the country of their birth when they go to walk

among the stars. Our dead never forget this beautiful earth, for it is the mother of the red man. We are part of the earth and it is part of us. The perfumed flowers are our sisters; the deer, the horse, the great eagle, these are our brothers. The rocky crests, the juices in the meadows, the body heat of the pony, and man—all belong to the same family."

Entry 46: Ten at night. Crummy motel. Nothing decent on TV. Sand storm blowing hard. Visibility near zero. Small town's shut down for the night.

Forgot to stop for supplies so dinner's a package of *Lance Cheese Crackers* and a handful of cashews, washed down with a room temperature can of *Arizona Green Tea*. Saving the lone remaining chocolate pudding cup for dessert later. I'd kill for a cold beer. Or a warm one, for that matter. Not a good night to pass with senses intact.

Not really sleepy, but should be. Long day out in the desert. Nose and forehead sunburned. Can't seem to completely wash the sand from my hair.

Need to find a Laundromat in the worst way. Two days past the last of my clean underwear, and all my socks are standing upright on their own. Maybe I should just toss out whatever's dirty and replace with new stuff picked up at the next *Walmart* I come to. Not a bad idea, actually. One potential problem. I wear the ultra-comfy *Nordstrom* house brand of jockey shorts, but still I suppose I could somehow manage to adapt to *Fruit of the Loom*. After all, desperate times call for desperate measures.

There are nights like this which can make me think I may have pulled out of the professional fast lane and retired too soon. Like every other baseball pitcher who ever lived,

I'm convinced I probably could have hung on for a few more productive seasons by trading my decelerating fastball for a decent changeup, or some other pitch requiring less spring to the arm. A *knuckler*, maybe.

Still, I suppose I should just accept the choices I made and be grateful I somehow survived years in the trenches without a ghastly wound. A few nicks and bruises, sure, a touch of malaria, but not much else, at least which shows.

Not all my friends were so lucky. I think often of a pair of journalistic colleagues, Bill Latch and Neil Davis, friends over at NBC who were gunned down by tank fire in a *tin-pot* coup attempt in Bangkok in nineteen eighty-five. I can still see the fury written on the face of Tom Brokaw as he broadcast news of the tragedy.

Bill and I were best friends, traveled extensively together, and knocked back many a beer on Bangkok's infamous Patpong Road. A geologist, Bill traveled from his native Colorado to Thailand for the adventure. He quickly integrated himself into the culture, learned the language, married a Thai girl, and fathered two children. Loved his life. Bill was thirty-five when he died. I miss him still. He was the friend I was destined to have remained close to across the decades. I feel cheated by his death.

The job description for every war correspondent really should contain the following warning:

This position is hazardous to your health and requires constant attention to detail to prevent bodily harm, which can include death. The position can trigger depression, anger, nausea, disgust, excessive sweating, profanity, sleeplessness, alienation, disruption of a normal family life, marital dissolution, profuse bleeding, and permanent disabilities of a nature too terrible to contemplate. Malaria is an ever-present risk, along with dengue fever, dysentery, heat stroke, foot rot, salmonella, snake and bug bites, as yet undiscovered bacterial infections, including those of the flesh-eating variety, and other conditions which could contribute to a complete meltdown of the immunological defense mechanism. Have a nice day.

The beginning of the end of my life as a foreign correspondent was determined one night in a remote South African farming community, Vedersdorp, the stronghold of the Afrikaners Resistance Movement, a paramilitary force led by a charismatic thug named Eugene TerreBlanche, a white supremacist who'd vowed a fight to the death if the government of President F.W. de Klerk continued to negotiate with Nelson Mandela on bringing an end to decades of apartheid.

TerreBlanche, who once had his henchmen pin me to a tree and pummel my rib cage with their fists simply because he hated journalists, was a farmer who not long ago was hacked to death by black workers in a pay dispute. I could call it divine retribution, but wouldn't think very much of myself if I did. Gloating over another person's death is not a place I want to visit, however tempting.

This particular evening TerreBlanche called out his *troops* when de Klerk helicoptered into town to challenge right-wingers in their own backyard by addressing a town hall meeting on the pressing need for a multiracial government before unrest tore the nation apart beyond all hope of repair. A courageous move.

I drove to Vedersdorp to cover what everyone was certain would develop into one hell of a news story.

It was clear from the outset the radical Afrikaners were itching for a fight, and had assembled in force, armed with hunting rifles and pistols. The government mustered an equal number of well-armed police to try to checkmate the hard-line nationalists. The two sides faced off yards apart on a side street two blocks from the town hall meeting.

While de Klerk spoke to a packed auditorium of well-behaved citizens, it doesn't take long for things outside to turn ugly.

The spark was a black man behind the wheel of a mini-bus who had the misfortune to turn onto the street of the faceoff and found himself in the middle of a howling pack of enraged whites. The mob descends on the bus, attempting to pull the poor man out. The driver panics and hits the accelerator, plowing through the tightly-packed crowd, mowing down people and, in the process, dragging the man standing right beside me under the wheels of the now runaway vehicle, ripping him to shreds.

One second I'm standing shoulder to shoulder with the young man, a curious farmer who drove to town to see the *show*, the next he is swept away. If we had exchanged positions, *I* would have been the one to die.

I attended the outdoor funeral at his farm a few days later. His black employees wept the hardest, collapsing to the ground, inconsolable in their grief. He was a well-loved family man who happened to be in the wrong place at the wrong time.

He wasn't alone.

As the young farmer is carved up, shots ring out. I turn to my right to say something to the man standing there. Only he's no longer there. He's crumpled at my feet, bleeding from a head wound.

All hell's breaking loose.

The police open up on the protestors, who return fire. I dive for cover behind a low rock wall. Then the tear gas. One canister lands a few yards away, spewing gas as it spins around. I gag, then dry heave.

A young man slides in beside me, his eyes wide with excitement, or maybe it was fear. Often difficult to tell the two emotions apart. They tend to overlap.

"You okay, man?" His concern is genuine. I assume he thinks I'm a fellow Afrikaner, or at the very least a supporter. God knows I look the part of an Afrikaner. Tall, bulky, bearded, fair-skinned, and green-eyed. Talk about *Central Casting*!

He offers me an old pistol.

I decline. The kid shrugs and moves on.

The police charge the protestors and it's then I see the only moment of sanity that night. A young white policeman is running down an equally youthful white demonstrator who is backtracking at high speed. The retreating man trips over a mound of dirt and falls, landing hard on his back just as the policeman arrives. They point their rifles at one another, barrels not a foot apart. No words are spoken. I hold my breath, waiting for someone to die, maybe both of them. Instead, the cop motions for the young man to move on, even offering a hand to help him rise to his feet. The outstretched hand is accepted.

Four people died that night. Dozens were wounded. It was the first time in decades of Apartheid that white police had killed white protestors.

That night was a watershed moment for me. I'd finally reached the saturation point for all the insanity and my thoughts began to linger on stepping aside for the young, eager *hot shots* impatiently waiting in the wings for an opportunity to show their stuff, just as I had years earlier. It was the natural evolution of things, as it always has been and always would be.

Although I hung on in Africa for two more years, including many dark months spent covering Angola's monstrous Civil War, I knew in my heart my time humping around Third World hellholes had all but come to an end. I'd seen it, done it, and wanted no part of it. I was forty-eight. That's considered young for many professions, but not always so much in mine. It was around then I set the wheels in motion to transition from battlefield to classroom. I felt it was my duty, my responsibility, to help prepare the next generation of journalists for what lay in wait for them.

I was comfortable then with my decision, and still am, except maybe on those dark and stormy nights in the middle of nowhere, all alone in a crummy motel room with nothing to eat but cheese crackers and a handful of cashews, and nothing good to watch on TV.

Entry 47: Stop for lunch at the *Roadkill Café*. Order the *Splatter Platter*, which sounds more appetizing than the *Swirl of Squirrel*. Skipped dessert.

Entry 48: Keeping a list of things which are getting on my nerves out here on the road:

- Gas stations charging a dollar for air.
- A long walk from a gas pump to the bathroom.
- *Talking* gas pumps.
- People pumping gas who share with the world the *Jay-Z* CD blasting out of their vehicles sound system.
- When I'm given a senior citizen discount without even asking for it.
- Being unable to cash in a ten dollar lottery ticket from Tennessee in New Mexico.

- Bugs which strike the windshield directly in my line of vision. They never impact a foot to the left or right, up or down, of where I'm focused. It's always smack in the middle, forcing me to slide down in the seat, or hike myself up, to see the road ahead. Using the windshield washer fluid only makes matters worse.
- Month-old road kill on the side of the road. Why municipalities allow these poor creatures to decompose in full public view escapes me. The body count of our furry friends who fail to survive an encounter with a multi-ton mass of hurtling metal is shocking. I'm surprised the humble squirrel has yet to be declared an *endangered species.*
- A high-speed encounter with a large bird which lodges itself in the car grill and requires a butcher knife to cut out.
- Highway debris. The roads of the country are a junk yard for anything which can be tossed out a car window, ejected from the bed of a pickup, fall from the sky, or blow in by the wind. Nearly hit a grandfather clock once. An actual anvil shredded my front right tire and chewed up part of the undercarriage. I replaced a windshield early on and the replacement is already pockmarked.
- Texting behind the wheel. Teens are in the forefront of this, but their parents do not lag far behind. I find myself hugging the white line on the shoulder of the road on a regular basis now to put a little more distance between myself and cars veering over the center line. It's an epidemic.
- No highway signage alerting me when I cross into a new *time zone.*

- You ever notice how long the lines have become these days at fast food drive-thru windows? I sometimes see fifteen, twenty cars strung out single file when inside the restaurant there's hardly a soul at the counter. Many is the time I've parked my car, walked inside, freshened up, placed an order, filled my cup at the beverage counter, sat down and ate a meal, topped off my drink, and then strolled back to my car only to recognize the same people sitting in line I saw when walking in. The American love affair with the automobile is quite something.
- Parents who think it's cute when their five-year-old son urinates in the end of the motel swimming pool where I happen to be.
- The shrinking size of candy bars. The smaller they are, the more expensive they've become. They were once nearly the length of my hand, but are now just marginally longer than my thumb. What once cost a dime is now a buck eighty in some convenience stores.
- Wardrobe decisions by *Walmart* shoppers, especially during the summer months when the discarding of clothing results in way too much exposed flesh for my sensitive nature.
- The explosion of tattoos. I find "body art" in general to be unattractive, especially those inked on a woman's arm, neck, or calf. Worst of all on a woman's breast. That's like drawing a mustache on the *Mona Lisa*.
- Missing my naps. A nap is a greatly underappreciated form of recreation. I consider naps worthy of praise, if not outright poetic verse. Anyway you approach it, a road trip is not conducive to maintaining a regular nap schedule. In optimum times, free from the demands of

the road, I'd take a ten minute pre-nap nap around ten and a leisurely nap in mid-afternoon. From time to time as I travel, I'm able to catch short snoozes at highway rest stops in the front seat of the car when heavy eyelids and mental drifting tell me it's prudent to shut down for a few minutes. Hardly refreshing, however, what with the awkward sleeping position in a small space already stuffed to the rafters, plus all the noisy truck traffic entering and exiting, and those well-meaning people, including state troopers, tapping on my window to see if the old guy slumped over the steering wheel is still alive.

- Motel TV remote controls with missing or dead batteries.
- The sound made by motel vacuum cleaners.
- Motel carpeting which turns my feet black.
- "Crunchy" motel bedspreads.
- Motels with broken ice machines.
- Discovering a *KFC* chicken leg left behind days earlier in a motel microwave.
- Car alarms shrieking in the middle of the night.
- The couple in the motel room next to mine engaged in exuberant sex at three in the morning.
- Motel toilets located more than an arm's length from the toilet paper holder.
- Motel toilet paper which doubles as sandpaper.
- Unidentifiable sticky stuff on the walls and floor of motel bathtubs and shower stalls.
- Motel shower stalls so small I have to step outside of them to turn around.
- Motel shower heads four feet off the floor, requiring me to wash my hair on my knees.

- Motel window curtains which fail to close all the way.
- Higher motel rates on weekends.
- Motel desk clerks who don't speak English.
- *Non-Smoking* motel rooms which are anything but(t).
- Motel rooms with no three-prong electric wall outlets.
- Motels which charge a fee for internet access.
- I miss the motel room key, an actual metal key. It's all about plastic cards these days with magnetic stripes which have a multitude of ways to malfunction, including when the card comes into near contact with a cell phone.
- Convenience store hot dogs. And suchi.
- Convenience store drink cups which are too large for my cup holders.
- Snakes in highway rest stop bathrooms. Baby rattlesnakes actually seek refuge there on chilly desert nights and the bite from these fingerlings can put you in the hospital.
- Highway work zones, especially those which are unmanned but still disrupt traffic flow.
- Coming upon closed highway rest stops when I need to *go* in the worst way. Quickly learned the importance of carrying around a *Mason Jar* with a tight screw-top lid for such emergencies. Guys are so lucky in this respect.
- Being stuck at a drive-thru ATM behind a person who waits until they get to the machine to start looking around for their card, follow that up with multiple slow-motion transactions, and then put everything back in order and check their hair and teeth before driving on.
- Driving with the sun in my eyes.
- Toll roads.
- Being unable to locate an English-language radio station.

- Those times when my GPS conks out in the middle of nowhere, leaving me stranded.
- Being stuck *behind* a heavily-laden truck creeping *up* a mountainside, in the fog, on a two-lane road, late at night.
- Being *tailgated* by a heavily-laden truck careening *down* a mountainside, in the fog, on a two-lane road, late at night.
- Tailgaters. I sometimes back them off with a dose of windshield washer spray. At speed, droplets of water can reach back a good thirty, forty feet, more than enough to make contact with the windshield of the person riding my bumper. This is a declaration of war, of course, and an exchange of hand gestures is inevitable. Yes, I'm eleven-years-old.
- Be careful, very careful, of women behind the wheel under the age of twenty-five. I'm surprised these aggressive, lead-footed young ladies do not dominate the *NASCAR* circuit. They would put the men to shame.
- The sound made by air brakes.
- Fingers turning orange when I eat *Cheetos.*
- Bicyclists who use the highway when a perfectly good bike path is a few feet away.
- Areas without NPR coverage.
- Paying a two hundred nine dollar traffic fine in Holbrook, Arizona, when I fail to see a stop sign planted *behind* a huge tree. Of course, a policeman just happens to conveniently parked across the street at that precise moment with ticket book in hand.
- And nothing irritates me more than coming over a rise and seeing the skyline of a city...

Entry 49: Half a day snarled in Sunday traffic waiting to cross Hoover Dam. Crawling towards the "man-made wonder" in a string of hundreds of cars lined-up single file on a narrow road carved out of a mountainside. Catch a glimpse of the dam every now and then far below in Black Canyon, but it's quickly swallowed by the next bend in the road.

Time to kill, but no readily apparent way to kill it. The radio's spitting static, can't phone the kids due to the impenetrable sheets of rock walls. Napping and reading are out, of course, and the last thing I want right now is to listen again to the *Bob Dylan Greatest Hits* CD, or any of the other *albums* I'm hauling around. Don't get me wrong. I love Dylan. The musical poet of my generation. But I've been playing his CD over and over again and worry I'll do something terrible if I hear him sing *Mr. Tambourine Man* one more time. Eat half the *Subway* tuna sandwich I'd picked up the evening before and stored overnight in the cooler. Holding the other half of the sub in reserve for later, provided the tuna's still edible by then.

Despite the traffic, actually a minor hiccup in the grand scheme of things, I must say the road trip's going well, even spectacular from time to time. Far better than I expected, that's for sure, although I have no reference point for it...but if the next leg of the journey is anything approaching what I've experienced so far, you'll hear no squawks from me.

Health's good, energy level's not bad, seldom bored or disappointed. Enjoying time spent behind the wheel. I always liked to drive. Thank God for that. Sleeping fine. Should be eating better, for sure. Far too many candy bars and chips, and those stale donuts which pass for breakfast in motel lobbies.

Stunning scenery every which way I look out on the road, and the people who populate the land are turning out to be a pleasant surprise. Easy smiles, polite, open. We're all pretty much alike when you take the time to navigate through and around all the bullshit and get down to core essences.

Winging it is working out fine. Still a *rush* not knowing what's waiting for me around the next bend in the road. Pretty much the only time I deviate from my pledge to keep it spontaneous is when I realize I'll be straying into areas heavily-populated by tourists, which means finding a motel room could be difficult, if not impossible, especially on weekends and holidays, so I go online and book ahead.

I certainly haven't been doing any *post-trip* planning of note so far. Long way to go before that's really necessary. Besides, I have more than enough on my plate right now to keep me focused and entertained. Still, it probably wouldn't hurt to give at least *some* thought to the making of a tomorrow. After all, tomorrow's where I'll be spending the rest of my life. Something to chew on. Maybe tomorrow.

I have, however, been thinking about compiling an actual *Bucket List*. Things left to do before I kick the proverbial bucket. Don't have one and maybe I should. A little laser- focusing in my life certainly couldn't do any harm. The project seems important to my generation as they leave their fifties behind and realize there's much left undone, and not all that much time to take care of business.

If nothing else, a *Bucket List* makes for an interesting, time-killing mental exercise, although I haven't been able to come up with much of a list so far. Maybe that's because of the life I've lead. Fortunate to have seen much, done much and, from time to time, maybe even leaving a path where not much of one existed before. On top of that, I just no longer have that old fire burning in my belly compelling me to chalk up a fresh string of dramatic endings. Let other people climb Mount Everest, rappel down skyscrapers, bungee jump, sky dive, base dive, free dive, go spelunking, swim with sharks, explore underwater caves, wing walk…

Still, I suppose I *could* come up with a thing or two. Nothing too dramatic or dangerous, of course. Don't want to risk making the evening news.

After a careful sorting through scores of options, I've discovered that residing at the very top of *my* very own *Bucket List*, holding the high ground over developing a liking for endives and cranberry sauce, bowling a 300-game, learning to play the tuba, and manning first base for the Yankees is…a dinner date with actress Jacqueline Bisset. Just one date and my life would be made, although I would be open to taking things to the next level if she absolutely insisted.

I've been smitten with Miss Bisset from the moment I first laid eyes on her when she popped-up in a small part in some sixties movie, and by the time she appeared in a wet t-shirt in *The Deep*, my goose was cooked…and although my goose certainly ain't what it used to be, it still doesn't mind roasting in a hot oven from time to time.

Jacqueline is easily the most beautiful woman ever, of course, but she's not without at least *some* competition. I *suppose* there are people out there who could make a case for Hedy Lamar, Eleanor Parker, Greer Garson, Ingrid Bergman, Catherine Deneuve, Michelle Pfeiffer, Toby Wing, Vivien Leigh, Kim Novak, Catherine Zeta-Jones, Elizabeth Taylor and, of course, Ava Gardner.

Ah, Ava. Just possibly *cousin* Ava. She was born in the Rural South on a farm just down the road a short piece from my grandfather's spread where long leaf tobacco and dewberries were grown side-by-side. I've been told Ava and I are likely related, although the bloodline is obscure, which is not uncommon on *Tobacco Road.* I overheard an aunt once say pretty much everyone in those parts was related one way or the other, but that it was generally unwise to examine the connections too carefully. Too many nasty family feuds began that way.

Ava was a product of her hardscrabble upbringing. She was an earthy woman, fond of going barefoot, even when she reached star status. Her language was salty and no nonsense and she lived life by her own rules. "I must have seen more sunrises than any other actress in the history of Hollywood," she once quipped. Ava proclaimed she wanted to die with a cigarette in one hand and a glass of whiskey in the other and she pretty much got her wish. Emphysema claimed her at sixty-seven.

I've often driven past the billboard on *I-95* advertising the Ava Gardner Museum in the town of Smithfield. I really must drop by one day to take a look. Maybe even try to get a family discount off the admission price.

Time is being consumed in great gulps as the line of cars continues its impossibly slow crawl towards Hoover Dam. People blowing horns to release frustration, leaving cars and darting behind boulders to relieve themselves. I can hear couples arguing, babies crying. Even laughter now and then. Drivers up ahead appear to have a "tailgate party" going.

A young man approaches and asks if I can spare some water. His daughter's not feeling well and is desperate for something to drink. I give him two pints of bottled water I retrieve from the rear of the hatchback. He offers to pay, but I turn him down. Water's water, but I hope others don't now descend on me.

Must say I'm actually enjoying this rare opportunity to casually amble about in my head. Lots of good memories out there I seldom revisit anymore. Not sure why that is.

Spent some twenty years living overseas. Quite a slice of my life. I suppose those were the happiest of times for me, at least the version of it I've settled on, and what I can remember of it, or allow myself to remember of it. Those memories mostly survive now as select morsels, mere shadows and echoes of what once was, and I wouldn't have it any other way. An abundance of memory only serves to dismay and confuse. At least that's been my experience.

The summer of my life was good, no doubt about it... the professional years solid and productive, buttressed by a unique camaraderie forged by fire. Certainly no shortage of good laughs along the way back then. We found humor—the more bizarre and alien in nature—an effective counterweight to the rigorous demands of our profession.

One good example of that takes us to Thailand. Women there may be the heart and soul of that ancient society, but have few rights under the law, at least back when I lived there. A Thai man, for example, could just kick his wife and children to the curb and pretty much not worry about legal and social repercussions...as long as he could sleep with one eye open. To drift off, to lose concentration if only for a minute, could lead to just about the most frightful thing imaginable—to every male ever born, at least. Women may have a quite different take on the subject.

In the late-seventies and early-eighties, abusive, philandering husbands in Thailand were under attack by wives hell-bent on exacting revenge by taking matters into their own hands, so to speak. That revenge took the form of using scissors, knife, hatchet, straight razors, or lids of tin cans, to actually lop off the penis of the unwary male as he slept or was passed out from drink. We're talking about the *actual* parting company of a man and his most treasured body part.

Thai newspapers, of course, were having a field day reporting on the epidemic, and paid special attention to the inventive ways women disposed of their *trophies*.

One woman, for example, tied her husbands severed penis to a helium-filled balloon and up, up and away it went. Where *it* returned to earth no one knows. The balloon was last seen swept up in air currents tracking in a northerly direction towards The Golden Triangle.

Then there was the woman who fed *it* to her duck. Another young lady tossed *it* into nest of voracious red army ants...and one woman wrapped *it* in a newspaper and tossed *it* through the open window of a passing bus heading out of town.

Then there was the young wife who dropped the severed penis into a septic tank. By the time *it* was recovered from the vile muck there was no hope of surgically re-attaching the wayward *willy*.

This particular man, according to stories floating around at the time, had no recourse but to go shopping for a new penis at a local hospital offering men replacement parts. His donor was said to be a man in the same hospital wing undergoing a sex change operation and no longer had need of his male privates. During post-op recovery, so goes the story, the man with the new penis visited the room of the donor to thank the now *her* and the two fell in love and, yes, eventually married.

Of course, there was no end of discussion in bars around Bangkok for the next few months of the disturbing images the honeymoon conjured up.

Hoover Dam. Haven't seen it in nearly an hour, but I'll assume it's still there. Would be nice to actually cross it before night falls. Hopes are not high.

The dam, of course, is named after the president who gave

the thumbs up to construction in nineteen thirty-one as the Great Depression dug in its heels across the battered land.

I actually saw Herbert Hoover once. I was around nine or ten. The former president was attending some event at the Tomb of the Unknown Soldier. Went there with my dad and little brother. I can actually remember Hoover walking ramrod straight, head thrust back, which served to exaggerate his substantial belly. Man moved with short, hurried strides, his demeanor no nonsense. He reminded me of a penguin in a hurry.

Now that I think about it, turns out I've seen my fair share of presidents, former presidents, and presidents-to-be in my life. My job, along with the years spent in Washington and abroad when I was a youngster, pretty much guaranteed that.

Crossed paths with President Eisenhower several times when Ike paid a state visit to Greece in nineteen fifty-nine. My dad was Public Affairs Officer at the American Embassy and responsible for helping make sure the circus went according to plan. Such an uproar preparing for the presidential visit. I remember thinking then how far too difficult adults made their lives, and promised I'd never allow that to happen to me.

Laid eyes on then Vice-President Lyndon Johnson in nineteen sixty-two as he drove down Pennsylvania Avenue in an open car with John Glenn, who'd just completed the first earth orbit by an American astronaut. Washington public schools had been let out for the day and I staked out a front row position at Fourteenth and Pennsylvania, a few blocks from the White House. The smile on LBJ's face was a mile wide, and genuine. He loved moments like that. Johnson could have gone down as a great one but for the way things got fouled up in Vietnam on his watch.

Then there was Richard Nixon. I covered the White House periodically over the years as vacation relief. I never liked the assignment and always tried to beg off. The section for the news media was cramped and stuffy. Little opportunity for actual information-gathering back then for anyone but the really big journalistic guns, like Dan Rather, the then *young prince* of broadcast news. I was envious of the guy. Handsome, making big bucks, always a beautiful woman or two nearby.

This was the *Watergate Era* and I had several opportunities to observe Nixon at that critical moment in his presidency. He was a defeated man by then, and it showed. Moved at a glacial pace, humped over, avoiding actual eye contact. His skin was gray and his suits baggy. I probably would have felt sorry for him had he not been engaged in all sorts of criminal enterprises.

I ran into Gerald Ford after he left the White House, a fleeting moment in a Washington hotel hallway as he strode into a political fund-raising event. Overheard him order an aide to "get me the hell out of here as soon as possible!"

Confess to not being a great admirer of Ford. It dated back a few years to when communist troops had encircled Saigon and Ford went on the air to announce American involvement in Vietnam was at an end. Must say that made those us still there a little nervous. Retribution from deservedly pissed-off South Vietnamese was always a distinct possibility. Their ultimate restraint was admirable. I'm not sure I would have been so magnanimous given similar circumstances.

Saw Bill Clinton for the first time in two thousand eight as he campaigned for Hillary in the North Carolina town of Lillington. Clinton gave a rousing, off-the-cuff speech from the porch of an old house, but his wife lost the state's Democratic Presidential Primary to Obama in a landslide.

Debated going up to Clinton and telling him my eldest daughter was once Chelsea's babysitter, but he was surrounded by gushing women, so I settled instead for a *Dr. Pepper* and plate of Carolina pulled pork barbeque.

To me, all of seven, John F. Kennedy was just a tall man in a white shirt tossing a tennis ball against a brick wall at our home in Tehran, who allowed me to retrieve the ball when it got away from him.

Kennedy was a lowly member of the House of Representatives when he stayed with us for a few days back in fifty-one, or thereabouts. As Press Attaché at the American Embassy, it was my father's responsibility to see Kennedy's wants and needs were taken care of. Why Kennedy stayed at our house and not in a hotel is lost to history. Conditions were certainly Spartan back then so maybe it was thought JFK's chances of staying healthy were better with us versus a lousy hotel with a suspect kitchen, although our own kitchen was hardly five-star, as he came to learn.

For decades afterwards, my mother enjoyed re-telling the story about Kennedy's final hour with us.

Kennedy had a flight out of Tehran at seven in the morning and my mother instructed our cook Ali to have breakfast on the table by five-thirty. When Ali failed to arrive (he was drunk and passed out in the garden), my frantic dad roused my mother from a sound sleep and asked what could be done about breakfast, meaning what could *she* do. She threw on a robe and jumped into action, like any good nineteen-fifties housewife.

To her horror, my mom discovered our two dogs had pulled the tablecloth to the floor, along with the dishes. She instructed the houseboy to clean up the mess and turned to the kitchen.

"We had a kerosene stove with four burners, but only one would light," she recalled. "The wicks were missing on the other three. I put on a percolator of coffee and found we had two eggs but no bread. While mixing flour, Crisco and baking powder for a *hoecake,* which I would fry in a black iron skillet, Kennedy walked into the kitchen and told me he had to run, and thanked me "for the good try."

The summer John F. Kennedy stayed with us was the year I received two copies of *Treasure Island* at my birthday party. Hardbacks with a colorful dust jacket of Long John Silver with a parrot on his shoulder and saber in hand. I remember spending many hours just staring at the image.

That was about the time my dog gave birth to a liter of sixteen on my bed as I slept. Imagine the surprise when I awoke to all those wiggling, sticky, wet bodies at my feet.

A few days later, my dad drowned half the pups. Stuck them in a burlap bag and held it under water in our swimming pool until the thrashing stopped.

My dad explained the mother could not feed such a large liter. "Better to save half, than lose all," he said. I never looked at my father the same way after that.

My dad was just forty-eight when he died. Stomach cancer... which took its time. Those were the days before chemotherapy and advanced radiation techniques. It was cut them open, cut out what they could, sew them back up, and hope for the best. My dad didn't stand a chance.

I can still see my father standing at the dining room window of our Washington home dressed in his light green pajamas and blue-gray silk robe, just staring at the snow falling on Massachusetts Avenue, his once robust body a mere shadow of what it had been. His thoughts were deep and far away, and I dared not intrude...although now I wish I had. So many questions left unanswered, so many words never spoken.

I sensed what a terrible, terrible waste this was. An ambassadorial appointment was in the works to an African country, and my dad was so looking forward to raising his beloved three-year-old daughter, Dede, who'd adopted our family when we lived in Greece.

This nightmare unfolded during the brutal Washington winter of sixty-one, in the weeks leading up to and after John Kennedy was inaugurated President of the United States.

Dad lived to see the new president take office, but slipped away one February afternoon at the Bethesda Naval Medical Center, spinning in bed in unimaginable pain, surrounded by nurses repeatedly jabbing his torso with morphine-filled hypodermic syringes because his heart was no longer strong enough the pump the pain-killer throughout his ravaged body. A savage way to die.

He and Kennedy are now buried not even two hundred yards apart at the Arlington National Cemetery—Kennedy at the foot of Lee Mansion with a spectacular view of Washington on the Potomac...my dad on a steep hillside overlooking hundreds of headstones of those who rest nearby.

My mother joined him there nearly forty years later, having never remarried.

I met Jimmy Carter in Zambia in nineteen ninety-one. He and Rosalyn were in West Africa as part of an international team assembled to monitor a presidential election, to make sure everything was on the up and up, at least by Africa standards, which were not very high to begin with.

Ran into the former president late one night in the hotel coffee shop. He was sitting alone, nursing a cup of something. No Secret Service anywhere in sight, at least that I could see.

I was on the hunt for a pack of cigarettes and didn't want to intrude on his thoughts. Our eyes connected as I was leaving and he motioned for me to come over and join him. I don't think he really wanted company, but may have disliked being alone even more.

Carter asked how I thought the national election campaign was going, if I'd seen any evidence of fraud. He somehow knew I'd interviewed President Kenneth Kaunda, recognized as one of the *Founding Fathers* of modern Africa, but who'd ruled under emergency decree from practically day one since he came to power in nineteen sixty-four.

The Zambian experience was so very African and just one more example how difficult it is to import western-style democracy to a continent divided by ancient tribal rivalries and things beyond the scope of our ability to comprehend.

Carter also wanted my "gut instincts" about Kaunda *the man*, who'd bowed to intense international pressure to hold free elections and was locked in a tough campaign, which he ultimately lost to a so-called "progressive" candidate who, years later, would become yet another iron-fisted African ruler. Such a predictable, sad, and frustrating cycle.

Carter was worried there was a risk Kaunda at the last minute would back down on his pledge to hold free elections and resume his authoritarian rule. I told the former president I thought Kaunda's day had passed and that the transition of power would be relatively smooth one. Kaunda, to me, appeared resigned to defeat and retirement. Carter happily agreed with my assessment.

The conversation was general in nature after that. I recounted the time I covered Rosalyn's visit twelve years earlier to refugee-swollen camps along the embattled Thai-Cambodian border back when she was First Lady. I didn't tell this to Carter, but I clearly remembered how the snow white pant suit Rosalyn wore that day stood in such sharp contrast to the unspeakable conditions in the camps.

The morning after our late-night encounter, Carter sent one of his aides to my room to see if I'd be interested in discussing a position at The Carter Center in Atlanta. I was flattered, but politely declined. I liked what I was doing.

Carter's a good man. Warm. Genuine. Too nice a guy for the job he was elected to do.

Nineteen sixty-eight. Ronald Reagan was taller than I thought he'd be, and beefier. His face was deeply-lined. His full head of hair had an orange tint to it. He was fifty-seven.

Reagan had flown into town for some political fund-raising event, and I was the sole reporter waiting for him when he bounded down the steps of his private plane. Just me and my veteran cameraman, Chris, who'd been a combat photographer during the Second World War.

I didn't know much about Reagan beyond he was governor of California, and had come up short in an attempt to win his party's presidential nomination. His face also popped-up on TV now and then late at night in old B-movies. That was pretty much the sum total of my knowledge of the man who would be elected President of the United States one dozen years down the road.

The old, savvy pro immediately locked onto the NBC logo on the film camera sitting on its tripod and strode over, even before I could request an interview. He shook Chris' hand, then mine.

Reagan looked up at the leaden sky. "Light's better if you stand there and I'll be here with the tarmac to my back, if that's okay?"

Without waiting for an answer, Reagan put his hands on my shoulders and swiveled me some ninety degrees to the left. "There we go." Properly positioned, he slapped his hands together and smiled. "Okay, what can I do for you?"

I'd been in television news for a short time, and at a small market network affiliate light years removed from the big leagues, so I was pretty much in the dark about every aspect of broadcasting, and hardly up on the issues of the day when I should have been.

When the camera rolled, I asked Reagan a softball question about why he was in town.

The second question to roll off my tongue was a doozy. Dumb as dumb could be. No, make that stupid! Knew it the moment it came out of my mouth. Reagan raised his eyebrows and smiled.

Humiliated, I dropped the microphone to my side, my chin slumping against my chest. To Reagan's great credit, he put me at ease with a warm smile and a pat on the back. "Can't tell you how many re-takes I had to do over the years," he said. "What about we start over again?"

That kind gesture meant the world to me, still does, and possibly kept me from abandoning journalism. The experience also taught me to never again get caught flat-footed.

To this very day, all these many years later, no bad-mouthing of Ronald Reagan around me ever goes unchallenged.

Entry 50: My hotel room's painted the color of money. And where's there's no green, there's glass. Great sheets of it. Outside the window stands a forty foot tall neon showgirl.

Las Vegas! No doubt about it...

Have landed in a downtown hotel once owned by gangster Bugsy Siegel, often credited for coming up with the idea of transforming a sleepy desert town into a gambling mecca. Of course, he was shot through the eye by his investors when the Vegas he envisioned was slow to develop. It was an unforgiving town then, and still is.

Nailed down the room on *Priceline* for twenty-two a night. That surprised even the desk clerk who checked me in, since rooms normally were in the fifty-sixty dollar range. The internet can be a money-saving tool, provided the timing is right. Twenty-two a night meant my timing was spectacular.

Entry 51: Spent the past week just looking around the city, feeding at the cheap casino buffets, and taking in the free nightly concerts at *The Fremont Experience,* a pedestrian mall with a blazing five block long light canopy and one half-million watt sound system. Nothing is done in moderation around here.

My first trip to Vegas. The life force is certainly infectious. The people-watching opportunities spectacular. Never thought much about it before reaching here, but we humans are really not very attractive physically, and most of the wounds are self-inflicted, especially in the hair, makeup and clothing departments. What could people possibly be thinking when conducting a self-examination in front of a full-length mirror just before they head out the door?

Anyway, enjoy walking around downtown after dark, admiring those iconic neon signs from the *ring-ding-a-ding* days when Sinatra's *Rat Pack* set the pace and tone around here.

A big effort's underway to rescue the early neon from the trash heap, and many are on display on a self-guided walking tour through downtown streets. The original *Aladdin's Lamp* neon sign is here, for example, along with the *Hacienda Horse and Rider,* among others, many I remember from old movies on TV.

Ocean's Eleven was the coolest film of the bunch, at least by nineteen sixty standards. Frank, Dean, Sammy, Joey, Peter, and crew. Those guys had their shit together. All the good-looking babes, the walk, the talk, the threads. Elvis wasn't bad either. *Viva Las Vegas* introduced me to the sublime Ann-Margaret, and for that I'm eternally grateful.

The old neon is best viewed at night, of course, when the bright colors overwhelm the senses, but that requires running a gauntlet of panhandlers, winos, hustlers, as well as swarms of forty dollar hookers offering blowjobs in the dark shadows. Not even tempted, thank you. The last thing I need is still further confirmation I'm slipping.

Entry 52: Visited Red Rock Canyon for the first time. The breathtaking two hundred thousand acre national conservation area out in the Mojave Desert gets its name from the red-colored sandstone formations embedded in the mountains of this valley, the color an important signpost for early wagon trains passing through the area. Difficult to believe all this magnificence is only thirty minutes from the Vegas Strip.

Park Rangers warn me to be on the alert for rattlesnakes should I venture off the marked trails...to "make a lot of noise" when tripping through the scrub or among the towering rock formations, home to herds of longhorn sheep and wild burros.

Taking their advice to heart, I belt out medleys from *West Side Story and Show Boat*, and the few numbers I know from

South Pacific. Don't see a single rattler. Even fellow hikers give me wide berth.

Entry 53: Some general observations about Vegas:

- It's against the law here to pawn your dentures.
- No skyline. Just huge signs.
- There are bail bondsmen, pawn shops, and wedding chapels on every other block.
- The neighborhood drug store doesn't sell books or magazines, but the condom section covers a substantial chunk of real estate.
- People playing the slots look like zombies, although I don't like insulting zombies.
- Every fourth person here works for a casino, escort service, or strip club, and the other three are their customers.
- I'd hate to try to grow a vegetable garden in this environment.
- Never eat or drink anything from your hotel room mini-bar. You'll quickly max out your credit card.
- Gambling here is a sure-fire way to get nothing for something.
- It would take three hundred fifty years for one person to spend the night in every hotel room in the city.
- I don't recognize the names of half the performers here getting top billing, which probably says more about my lack of knowledge of the modern music and standup comic scenes than the booking practices of the casinos. I know Cher, of course. Donnie and Marie are also in town. Celine returns soon. Read when she's in Vegas casino revenue jumps by five percent *everywhere* in

town. Given the volume of gambling here, that's a huge amount of money.

- Avoid blackjack tables where the dealer's an Asian woman. They're tough, and very, very good.
- Casino buffets are excellent laxatives.
- Vegas thinks of itself as spontaneous, but it's not. Everything is meticulously planned to laying hands on your very last dollar.
- If you have a weakness, it'll be exploited here. Your strengths, too.
- If you plan on leaving Vegas with a small fortune, go there with a large one.
- Never believe a casino when it tells you its slots are "the friendliest in town."
- The women around here sport more tattoos than the men.
- Seeing lots of people pushing grocery carts.
- I've never seen so many people trying so hard to have fun.
- The only way to stay solvent in Vegas is to never show up in the first place.

Entry 54: Drift on down to the actual Vegas Strip. Been avoiding it. No place to park, chock-a-block with humanity, the churning noise grating. Still, not to visit the infamous four-mile stretch of Las Vegas Boulevard would be an egregious violation of my road trip covenant. *See it all, do it all...even if I really don't want to.*

Wander into a casino. Win nine hundred dollars in twenty minutes at a ten dollar minimum blackjack table. Nice-looking woman in a cage cashes in my chips and asks what I plan to do with "all" the money. I ask if she'd like to help me spend it. She thinks that "sounds like fun." I like her, she likes me. All good-natured. Not at all mercenary. Or weird. Just Vegas.

Meet up with her later for dinner at what passes in Vegas as a "cozy" restaurant. One hundred tables, bright lights, kitchen clatter, high volume canned music, casino drone...

Wanda's in her fifties and takes care of herself. Six feet tall. Originally from Atlanta. Moved to Vegas soon after high school and became a showgirl where she put all those childhood ballet lessons to good use. Married a dentist from back East she met at a convention party and began a new life outside Philadelphia, in Berks County. Had twins, a boy and a girl. They were off on their own now. So was she after a divorce five years earlier. Returned to Vegas because she wanted a dramatic change of scenery, and some friends from the good old days were still around. Received a nice divorce settlement but took a casino job to stay busy. Had recently accepted a job offer in the human resources department of a casino in Reno. Reporting for work there next week. Less hectic and more traditional in Reno, she says, and her age isn't a liability.

"Vegas is a town for young people, not old broads like me. Anywhere else I'd be on the sunny side of middle age. Not here. Reno draws an older crowd so I'll fit in better up there. I also like Reno weather more than this place and Lake Tahoe's nearby for skiing...Planning on buying a nice condo. Maybe even a house with a pool. Real estate's in the dumps right now, so I know I can make a great deal. Looking for three or four-bedrooms for when my children visit and, eventually, grandchildren. Yes, I should be just fine. In fact, I should have made the move long ago, but time has a way of slipping by us. It all passes so quickly, doesn't it?"

Wanda invites me to her high-rise apartment for "a great view of the *Strip*." The furniture movers have already cleared out the place. All that remains is a folding lawn chair and an inflatable mattress.

Entry 55: My *first time* ever was at summer church camp, in a chapel, with a girl from Poughkeepsie named Cheryl.

That fumbling, seminal moment so long ago deep in the woods of West Virginia one starry August night lasts only a few minutes, if that, but made it crystal clear to me women would forever have my undivided attention. In retrospect, that was pretty much a no-brainer. After all, what's not to like? Women are intelligent, clever, witty, fun, tender, affectionate, nurturing, smell nice, and possess all the really neat body parts.

Yet in all my exposure to the wonderment that is woman, I must confess that in all likelihood I've never *fallen* in love as far as I can tell, although I sure as hell *stepped* in it big time every now and then. Two marriages and a string of long relationships are proof enough of that. Oh, I'll concede that more than once I *thought* I was in love, the love poets glowingly write about, but that was mostly back in my younger days when the sight of a bare breast led me to utter words one normally associates with being in love.

Then again, it's quite possible I really *was* in love from time to time, but had such unrealistic expectations for love, wanted far too much from it, I was simply unable to recognize love when it came calling.

There are times I'm convinced God is punishing me for that carnal indiscretion in that chapel pew so long ago, His wrath translating into a long procession of women moving in and out of my life, while denying me a forever bonding. Now I suppose some of you would argue that a plethora of women is not a curse, and I can see how you'd think that, but this inability to lock in an enduring relationship has been known to transport me to dark places from time to time.

As a substitute for *true* love over the decades, and to keep my spirits up, I often took temporary refuge in *flash romances*. Intense, carefree eruptions of varying duration which *never* involve joint checking accounts, in-laws, and lawyers. I also get to keep my "stuff" when all is said and done.

Marriage, of course, also has obvious upsides. Just ask any married person. They're quick to describe marriage as a wonderful *institution*, Yes, I'm sure that's true, provided you don't mind living in an *institution*. It's well-documented married men live longer than single men...even if they don't want to. While not a prerequisite, marriage has been known to play a role in perpetuating the human species. That's a pretty big deal. A guaranteed companion on national holidays is another important benefit, along with a regular sex life, at least in the early stages of marriage...and you'll get no argument from me that a legally sanctioned union is preferable to spending a night in Newark.

All kidding aside, it wasn't all that long ago I noticed many aging single friends, and some *not* so single, were going on the internet in an attempt to make a *cyber-connection*. Since everyone seemed to be doing it, and a few even reported some success, I decided to go for it. I'm a gambler and risk-taker by nature so I thought this had the potential to be interesting, enlightening, maybe even fun...and I never strayed far from the notion that maybe *she* was waiting for me out there in *cyberspace*, no more than a simple *mouse click* away.

So I signed up with an internet dating site and waited for the magic to happen...

Drove nearly four hours to get there. Long way to travel to

meet a person I've never met and know only in passing from several carefully-crafted sentences in her online dating profile, along with a few email exchanges.

I remember the night was clear, the moon was yellow, and the gentle breeze carried the scent of magnolia blossoms.

Must say I look pretty good, for me. New, expensive silk shirt from Saks, a day-old forty dollar hair style, a nice tan, body bathed in musk oil. I even had the hair stylist trim my eyebrows. I'm feeling loose and relaxed. A nothing ventured, nothing gained approach to life has generally served me well up to now and I have no reason to believe things were about to change.

The venue's a wine bar. An ideal neutral setting of her choosing in her hometown for a first meeting. I'm there ten minutes early to get the lay of the land. Lots of chrome and glass, and earth tones. Good lighting. Nice place.

Enter my date, right on time at the stroke of seven. She looks somewhat like the photos she posted on the dating site, enough so I can at least recognize her. I'd been warned that's not always the case.

Fifty-one. Tall, thin, graceful. Height of fashion. Turns out her family owns half the business properties on Main Street.

As she approaches the table, I instantly see in her eyes she's *not* at all impressed with me. Many decades in the social and professional trenches spanning multiple cultures has given me a heightened sense of when I'm not making the grade, and this is one of those times. My heart sinks a bit at the realization, but manage to hold it together and swallow the disappointment. Okay it happens, I tell myself. Grin and bear it. Have a drink, hope for some pleasant conversation, say goodnight, retreat to the motel, and head back home in the morning. No harm, no foul.

Then again, *maybe* I could win her over with my charm and wit. It's worked before. Over the years I've honed some pretty slick moves to capture the hearts of top-of-the-line women. It's what guys with average looks must do to have any hope at all of riding the high country.

First thing out of her mouth as she sits: "You look heavier than in your photographs online. I hope you don't have a flabby belly under that shirt. I really do not like men with paunches."

I decide to park the charm and wit.

Her voice is high-pitched and whiney. Fingernails raking across a chalk board. My testicles dive for cover.

I suppose I should let the remark pass with a polite smile, or reassuring words, but that's not me. Not by a long shot. She'd thrown down the gauntlet and was asking for it.

I lift my shirt, exposing my hairy belly. Not six-pack abs, but not too bad either, especially for someone my age.

She doesn't bat an eye at the hairy landscape and launches into pseudo-scientific babble that advances the proposition that *less* body hair translates into a higher IQ. I battle the temptation to show her the hair blooming on my shoulders.

As she drones on and on, I notice she has no lips. None whatsoever. I've never seen anything like that before. I'd remember if I had.

The downhill slide accelerates.

The wine steward approaches. His obligatory smile vanishes when he sees my companion. I'm confident he's met her before.

Five minutes later she's still meticulously pondering her choice, muttering at the limited selection of French wines and "over-stocking" of domestic offerings. The poor man is shifting his weight from leg to leg, looking at me with sad eyes.

The wine arrives. She takes a sip (without asking) from

my glass of California pinot noir, her face contorts, and she begins to expound at length on the superiority of French vintages.

I somehow manage to interject that many well-versed connoisseurs now consider California wines at least equal, and often superior, to those of France. She calls such people "idiots" (using the French pronunciation of the word, of course) and looks at me like a glob of dog shit stuck to her heel.

Now, this is the time most guys would normally bail, just stand up and leave, but Southern manners instilled in me from an early age compel me to hang around and subject myself to further abuse. I also sense I'll enjoy telling this story in the years ahead when recounting my sojourn into the world of internet dating, so it's imperative for me to find out how this night ends, even if it hurts.

My date's hungry and clearly determined to milk this encounter for all it's worth. So, there I am being pulled along in her wake as she struts across the grassy *Commons* to a restaurant with starched white tablecloths and an equally starched staff.

She orders a glass of champagne, then a bottle of wine, imported, and follows up with an exotic off-menu entrée. My debit card is haemorrhaging.

The more she drinks, the more vociferous the broadsides against the men she's dated, and there have been many, mostly doctors it seems for some reason. All have attention deficit disorders, she claims, and are unable to commit to a long-term relationship.

The bulging veins in her neck remind me of an Italian road map.

I feign shock at the revelation men are not falling at her

feet, along with hearing her third marriage (to a psychiatrist!) lasted only four months.

She orders an off-menu desert, and liqueur. Time is interminable. She begins to speak in slow motion. My legs fall asleep. I develop facial tics. The restaurant has emptied out. The wait staff's restless and wants to shut down the place for the night. My thoughts are focused on making it back to the motel room in time to catch a *History Channel* documentary on the *Bataan Death March*.

I finally manage to pry her away from the table and escort her to her car parked two blocks away. It seems like miles. I take up my customary curb-side escort position. My date immediately starts ranting against the tradition of men walking on the outside of women. "Women do not need to be protected by men!"

I elect not to squander what little remains in my tank explaining the tradition dates back centuries to pre-indoor plumbing days in Rome when people disposed of their body waste by tossing it out the window and onto the street. It was the women who would get splattered, not the men. I so wished at that moment to be in ancient Rome.

We reach her car. Mercedes, of course. Brand new, of course. Two-seater sports model.

As she climbs behind the wheel, she forces a half-smile (more of a grimace, actually). Her voice is glacial. "Well, have a good rest of your life."

My response as I close the car door: "My life will get a lot better in about five seconds."

Entry 56: Breakfast at *Denny's*. Two eggs over hard, bacon, grilled potatoes, double order of grits, and a Diet Coke.

Vegas is behind me now and I find myself in yet another

nameless small town. This time way out in the Mojave. Autumn's set in and there's a chill to the air. Snow's fallen on the highest peaks off in the distance.

Spot a *dust-devil* burst into life in the field across the street from the restaurant, kicking up sand and slinging around assorted lightweight debris, then vanishing as quickly as it materialized.

Walk out to the middle of the main drag. A whole lot of nothing every which way I look. The middle of nowhere in the middle of nowhere, all in the center of a town.

I'm back on the road by nine, heading north by northwest, no particular destination in mind...

Entry 57: I wish this place had a better name, one befitting its rawhide demeanor. Beatty sounds like the name of a town in Rhode Island instead of a rugged, untamed outpost in a far corner of the Mojave Desert at the doorstep of Death Valley.

Find a room at the *Atomic Inn*, drawing its name from the nuclear bomb testing which went on around here in the nineteen-fifties. Will be interesting to see if the streets glow at night.

Motel's just fine. Clean. Roomy. Quiet. Even has a micro-fridge. Reason to rejoice.

Late now. I'll check out the town tomorrow, all four or five blocks of it. Plan on hanging around here for at least a week.

Entry 58: Awaken to a rare rain falling in the desert, and all the surrounding peaks, barren yesterday, are now covered in snow. I'm at thirty-three hundred foot elevation in town and dodged the snowfall by maybe one thousand feet, but hear that snowline may drop down to here tonight.

The lousy weather's turned me off to the idea of driving

to check out Death Valley today, so I'll use the opportunity to look around here. That shouldn't take long.

Downtown Beatty stretches about one-half mile in the north-south direction, and one-quarter mile east to west, but that's a rough estimate. Let's just say it's small. Beatty's located at the eastern entrance to Death Valley, and this Nevada town depends on the tourist trade to help keep afloat. Things are clearly not going all that well in this down economy.

Just off the main drag, clusters of old rusted trailers and limp prefabs with neglected lawns. Weary-looking storefronts, shuttered businesses, damaged and rotting billboards clutter "downtown" and, on the fringes, out in the desert, four low-end brothels, all perfectly legal under state law.

I count at least five motels here, an equal number of no-frills meat and potato restaurants, two gas stations with attached convenience stores. There's no standard supermarket, but I came across a candy store, an ice cream parlor, and there's a small casino at the *Wagonwheel Motel*, where most of the *action* in town appears to be centered. There's also a cottage industry in venison, elk, and buffalo jerky, along with desert honey and stuffed olives, sold in a skid row of shops as you enter town from the south.

I ask the girl working the cash register at a convenience store where I could buy an apple around these parts and was told I'd have to drive forty miles to find one.

Take breakfast at some joint. Order a cheese and mushroom omelet. The side order ham steak's so large it flops over the sides of its own considerable platter.

Thirty-something cook comes out of the kitchen to ask how I like the food. I'm the sole customer so he pulls up a chair. I don't mind. Company's always welcome.

Man asks where I'm from, of course, then quizzes me about

"back East." Tells me he has a cousin in Roanoke, Virginia, who manages a tire store. Thinking of moving there himself. Says there's not much of a future in Beatty. "Everything's fouled up every which way you look," he growls, "including my life! Old lady took off with my kid, and car. Cleaned out the checking account and stole the flat screen TV. Even short-sheeted our bed."

Young waitress comes over and tries to pour me a cup of coffee, despite the fact I've told her twice already I don't drink the stuff...

Drift into a saloon in the early afternoon. Load up on local color dished out by *good old boys* hanging out at the bar. Most around my age, a few older, some considerably, with apparently nothing better to do than mix it up with old friends over a cold one on a cold day.

They accept me into the inner circle as if they'd known me forever. I suspect what they're really after is some new blood so as not to be forced to listen to the same old stories rehashed over and over again. The flaw with that plan is I'm there more to listen than talk, but manage to contribute enough fresh material to keep them happy. Buying a round for the house firmly cements my acceptance.

Ray: "Nobody around these parts made a fuss about the bomb testing going on back then. No bitching about fallout, and all the other bad stuff. Deformed babies, and that crap. It was just the way things were. Seemed necessary enough considering what was going on in the world at the time. Most folks were *busting buttons* we could do our patriotic bit to keeping the country safe."

A guy hard at work trying to dislodge a stubborn piece of

meat with a toothpick joins in: "Sure glad we never had to use those bombs for real. None of us would be here if we did. The Russians would have seen to that for sure."

Man named Frank: "Hell, an A-bomb going off on Main Street would have improved the looks of the town."

Laughter.

Bar chatter drifts to hush-hush goings-on out at the infamous *Area 51*, the world's most secret military base where, according to UFO theorists, and half the men at the bar, humans have long been interacting in assorted and sordid ways with extraterrestrials, both dead and alive.

Old man named Joe: "I know that shit's going on."

Me: "What makes you think that?"

Joe: "Why else the government so tight-lipped? Why not come right out and deny it?"

Me: "I thought it did."

Joe: "Nope, never did in any official way that I recall. Just ignores the whole thing. I'll tell you if people learned they got aliens and spaceships out there, they'd go ape shit."

Me: "You telling me the secrecy is for our own protection?"

Joe: "Sure looks that way to me. Just good old common sense."

A bearded man named Carl breaks his silence. "I say if bad stuff were really going out there, we'd have heard lots about it. You can't keep secrets that long. What's it been fifty, sixty years? More? Hell, government men can't keep something that big hushed up that long, much less a single day. Somebody would have spilled the beans, for sure. It's all bullshit. No doubt about it."

The bartender: "You'll think different when you wake up some morning and a green alien with a nasty attitude is in bed with you."

Carl: "Hell, I got that already!"

Takes a full minute for the laughter and back-slapping to subside.

I get the *skinny* on the brothels around here. People take them in stride. No outraged indignation I can see. A welcome revenue stream as far as the guys at the bar are concerned, and possibly a social diversion from time to time, although no one will admit to it.

Being the intrepid journalist I am with an insatiable appetite for comprehensive and accurate reporting, I press ahead and quiz my bar pals.

"So, what are those places like?"

Ray (light-hearted): "Ask Frank. He spends enough time there."

Frank (not happy): "Bullshit!"

Ray: "Bet old Frank has a discount card. He's in and out of the *Bikini* all the time. Girls there call out to him by name when they see him on the street in town. Girls from *Angel's Ladies*, too."

Frank: "More bullshit!"

Me: "Anyone know the going rate at those places?"

Ray: "Frank?"

Frank: "Why you asking me?! How the hell would I know that?"

Ray: "Then what do you *think* it probably is?"

Frank: "Well, I once heard some truckers talking about it. Seem to remember they said it was two hundred, two-fifty, for half an hour, or maybe it was fifteen minutes."

Ray: "Fifteen minutes! Hell, takes me fifteen minutes just to take off my socks!"

Entry 59: Hit the road at dawn, heading for Death Valley. An hour or so drive from Beatty.

Take a two-lane road cutting through the desert, then some low, barren hills. Cross into California, nearly missing the small wooden marker identifying the state line. Sun's climbing behind me.

Reach a rise and spread out below me is the white floor of the vastness called Death Valley. I pause to snap a few wide-angle lens photographs before continuing down the side of a long, gently sloping mountain. Ears pop as I pass through fifteen-hundred feet. Still a long way left to go before the road levels off and I find myself standing on the lowest and hottest crust of earth on the North American continent.

Temperature in this furnace once reached one hundred thirty-four degrees, just a fraction of a degree off the world record held by someplace in Libya. One twenty is common here. Early settlers had good reason to name this one hundred twenty-mile long basin Death Valley. It's more than deserving of its name. Mercifully, the temperature today is in the fifties.

Trouble breathing. Air's so damn thick below sea level. Like trying to suck honey through a straw. Have spent so much of my road trip thousands of feet above sea level where the air is thin and elusive, it's now slapping me in the face.

Hike way out in the salt flats. Bad decision. Biting wind whips up and pushes me around at will. Blowing salt stings my face and eyes are burning. Fingers stiffen in the cold. Camera takes a real beating. Will take forever to clean the lens and fragile sensor. Not fully confident the camera can be salvaged.

At first glance, you would think nothing could possibly

survive out here, but that's an illusion created by the withering sun and parched earth. There's indeed life. Not much, but some.

Park Ranger tells me plants here endure through an ability to absorb and store for long periods what little water may come available, and animals persist through a subterranean existence, or encased in shells or thick, hard hides as armor against the blast of heat and all its consequences. The tiny kangaroo rat doesn't drink a single sip of water in its lifetime. Not one. All the water it needs to survive is metabolized from the dry seeds it eats.

Death Valley's certainly not the place to overestimate your endurance or underestimate the determination of those rippling, wind-whipped sand dunes, mud-stone hills, and jagged canyons to do you harm. Place names here like Devil's Hole, Furnace Creek, Funeral Peak, Badwater, and Dante's View are not figments of someone's literary imagination.

Death Valley. No further proof needed God has a sense of humor.

Entry 60: Overheard someone actually use *"rootin-tootin"* in a sentence. Hardly a day passes, however, when some lame brain caught up in the Wild West atmosphere doesn't cut loose with a full-throated *"yippee ki-yay, motherfucker."* Can thank Bruce Willis for that.

Entry 61: Most people I meet on the road tell me quite a bit about themselves, often without realizing it, but there's a breed of men out in the high desert living off grid...rugged, solitary, reticent, hard men balanced on the fringe of society who don't want to be found.

Today I found one of them.

I set out from Beatty at first light heading into California on a day trip to take a look at the towering sequoia trees, a survivor from the time two hundred million years ago when early dinosaurs roamed the land.

Drive non-stop across Death Valley, and take dead aim on the Sierra Nevada, its snow-capped peaks looming ahead.

Two hours down the road I stop at the *Welcome Center* in a pretty village nestled at the foot of a mountain and ask the staffer on duty if there are any sequoias close by.

"If by close you mean six hours, then yes," the middle age woman informs me.

"Six hours! Did you say six hours? If I continued driving west for that long, I'd be well on my way to Hawaii."

"Sequoias are located on the western slopes of the mountains, the Pacific side," she instructs me with practiced precision. "You're on the east side, and there's no road over the mountains that'll take you straight there. If you were a bird, you could be there in twenty minutes, but since you don't have wings as far as I can tell, you'll have to drive down to Indian Wells, then catch *178* over to Isabella Lake. From there, go due north and you'll reach the park entrance, probably around dark. Maybe you can find a motel room, but they're no guarantees. It's Saturday, and lots of people drive over for the weekend from around Bakersfield. Sorry."

So much for the sequoias.

I retrace my tire tracks to Beatty, consoling myself with the knowledge on the return leg I'll at least be treated for the second time today to those dramatic landscapes. Actually, it'll be like seeing it all for the *first* time because scenery is pretty much all new when approached from the opposite direction. Didn't really think much about that until I started viewing things in a whole new light once I had a serious camera in my hands. On walkabouts, I make it a point now to glance back over my shoulder from time to time. Some of my best photographs have come that way.

When my blood sugar suddenly drops—my hands tremble slightly and I feel light-headed—I pull off on a dirt road for a bite to eat. Food always does the trick. Brought along a block of cheddar cheese, crackers, a *Hershey's Bar*, and a small bottle of cranberry juice for just such an *emergency*.

The supplies would also come in handy should I flip the car into a ditch out in the middle of nowhere and go undetected and unreached for several days. I've taken to heart those horror stories of people who'd been stranded in the emptiness and were forced to drink their own urine, or worse, to survive, if they survive.

I started carrying around emergency supplies back when I was a foreign correspondent. Breaking trails through the darkest corners, I quickly became aware of the foolishness of traveling empty-handed. No drug stores or supermarkets out there. Hospitals, either. While there was nothing I could do about a bullet with my name on it, a big cat leaping out of the bush, or a land mine snapping to life underfoot, I took control where I could. I'd usually tote along protein biscuits, peanuts, and candy bars, along with select medical supplies—antibiotic ointments, a tourniquet, salt pills, anti-malarial tablets, and pretty much any and everything which held out even a remote hope of providing fast, effective relief from runaway diarrhea. I was a popular guy with travel companions when the suspect meal we recently consumed insisted on making a quick and dramatic exit from the body, and was none too particular which orifice it used in the escape.

No sooner than I spread out my little meal on the hood of the *Mazda,* a lone gust of wind carries in grit which settles on the cheese, but I no longer mind all that much. An occupational hazard.

A few bites into my meal, the wind suddenly picks up...a furious sweep of air barreling down the hills, through the canyons. Great unions of tumbleweed bounce over the landscape like balls in a *Bingo Wheel.* It turns dramatically colder. The quality of light shifts on its heels, going from placid to dark and brooding. I gather up the food and retreat to the security of the car.

Some hours still left before it gets dark so I decide to explore this lonely dirt road which heads off into a vast, hilly, desert wilderness. It has to lead someplace. Why else would it even be here? Then again, I've been fooled before.

Don't get far before it begins to sleet. Windows fog up. Slush brushed aside by the wipers accumulates at the edges of the windshield. Visibility erodes fast. I debate turning tail, but convince myself to keep going, if just for another mile or two. Always another mile or two. That could easily be the inscription on my tombstone.

Within a few minutes I outdistance the squall and, topping a rise, stretched out before me is what I would loosely define as a town. From a distance, it looks deserted. Colorless. Stone cold dead. I suspect I just may have stumbled on a ghost town. They're not all that rare in this forsaken country.

I head for it.

The most prominent feature is the steep hillside blanketed in dozens of dilapidated wooden shacks with doors hanging by a single hinge, windows blown out, roofs sagging or caved in. Rusted and desiccated heavy machinery is scattered about. Off to my left, a shattered smelter. To the right, an overgrown cemetery with primitive wood crosses and sand-blasted headstones tilted at ugly angles. Framing the main road through town worn out houses, most still largely intact.

Then I spot a black *Jeep Wrangler* parked outside a house with a large wind chime hanging from a hook on the front porch, its metallic tinkling intruding on the silence. I catch a whisper of smoke rising from the chimney. Since no one comes out to *welcome* me to town, I waste no time in driving on.

Seeing pickup trucks parked here and there. Four or five of them. The wind carries in the bark of a distant dog, but I see no people. Not a soul. I do, however, sense eyes on me, and catch the slight movement of a chintz window curtain.

Somehow manage to convince myself to drive deeper into the town, a quarter-mile to the T-junction.

Leave the car to look around. The most prominent building is made of wood and rectangular in shape. A weathered sign nailed above the double door reads *Dance Hall*. An old Elvis Presley poster is taped to a window.

I pivot and face the long since closed post office now sagging in the middle, forming somewhat of a swayback shape when you look at it head-on. I know it once served as the post office because of the faded, hand-painted sign hanging just above the still-serviceable, and quite valuable, antique front door with its five small panes of beveled glass inlaid in a fan-like fashion across the top section. I know an interior decorator who'd kill to get her hands on that door. The two large storefront windows are boarded up. Layered generations of blue, red and yellow paint peel in unison from the exterior walls. An early hand-cranked gasoline pump is planted in the ground just to the right of the one-step-up porch, its glass dome in near mint condition, but the yellow metal base is rusting away and leaning ominously to one side.

Nearly fly out of my shoes when a dog slips up behind me and sniffs at my pant leg. Strangest-looking dog I've ever seen. The head and torso of a German Shepherd supported by squat Bassett Hound legs. Its breathing is shallow and wheezy, and the animal's snorting through a muzzle choked with snot.

A bearded man of about fifty, dressed in jeans and a bright yellow ski jacket, holds the leash. He's quite short, but solidly built. Chiseled features, cold blue eyes. Hair hacked to the scalp. One tough-looking customer. I wouldn't want to fuck with this guy.

"This was quite a town back a hundred years or more ago," he volunteers. "Silver mining, mostly. Made some people rich, but most people just ate dirt like they always do. Place's not so much to look at now, but I guess you can see that plain enough."

He seems okay so I feel less like a trespasser...and potential victim.

His dog is now stretched out on her side in the middle of the road, half asleep.

"She has a metal pin in her leg. Can't stand for too long. Fell into a hole. These old places can be very dangerous. No telling where you can end up if you're not careful where you step, and there's pretty much no one around to hear your cries if you screw up."

He glances at my car tags. "You're quite a long way from home."

Seeing I'm from out-of-state appears to put him somewhat more at ease. I introduce myself and we shake hands. His grip is vice-like and I wince. Name is Lucas. At least that's what he tells me.

I gesture at the decaying remains of the town. "So, people actually *do* live here now?"

"This is home to about fifteen of us." He then smiles. "But it can climb to twenty-five in the *tourist season*."

The evidence of a sense of humor allows me to relax a little more.

"So, how long you been living here?"

"Oh, a long time, I suppose. It's easy to lose track of time in this place. Besides, measuring the passage of years is not important as it is in *your* world."

A pickup truck passes a street over and the driver honks and waves. Lucas waves back.

"Henry, an undertaker two towns over. Visits his mother's old place from time to time just to see if it's still standing. She died about twenty years ago. He brings flowers to her grave every time he visits. Seems like a waste of good money to me. Wind blows them out into the desert as soon as they're laid there. Still, I suppose it's nice to be remembered. Not everyone one of us is so fortunate."

"How'd you end up here, if you don't mind my asking?"

He thinks for a moment. "So long ago," he says wistfully, "I almost don't remember myself. Not very interesting, I'm sure. I try not to dwell on the past. Can't see there's anything to be gained from it."

He reaches down and strokes the dog, which feebly wags its tail.

"I suppose I'll have to put her down soon. Shooting her will not be easy. I'd ask someone to do it for me, but she deserves I pull the trigger. Better she gets it from a loved one, don't you think?"

"What's her name?"

"Never actually got around to naming her. Doesn't really need one. Not out here."

Lucas clearly has a story to tell, and a damn good one, but he's not about to tell it to me. That's clear. No clever tricks I learned in the business of getting people to open up can win out over a person determined to say as little as possible. I decide not to press the matter. Instinct tells me uncovering the deep past about a guy like this could lead down a road I'd just as soon not travel.

Easy to tell the guy's educated. And I detect a faint trace of what could be a New England accent. There's little doubt in my mind something dreadful surely happened which led him to this dead end out in the desert. A broken heart, perhaps, or violent act...maybe both, colliding in some twisted, explosive moment, instantly regretted and deeply-mourned, but irreversible and life-altering.

"The solitude here's quite something," I observe, shifting into a lower gear. "Must be difficult at times."

"We all do what we have to do. It's not always easy. This life's certainly not for everyone."

"How so?"

"Well, just look at the place," he laughs. "Don't know many people who'd find this life appealing. Do you?"

"No, I guess not, but you seem to be getting along fine."

"My life's pretty basic but I'm used to it. Besides, I never wanted much. Never expected much. Have just a fireplace and wood stove for my heat and cooking. Scavenge for wood, but there's plenty of it around. Well water tastes a little bitter, but it doesn't bother me so much anymore. Hunting's not bad if you're a decent shot. Rabbits, quail, some larger game. You'd be surprised how little it actually takes to get by. I do miss hot showers, however. I won't deny that. I try to get to town every few weeks for one. Lady friend lets me use her shower, provided I scrub her back, of course."

"Of course," I smile. "So, how do you manage to follow what's going on in the outside world?"

"What makes you think I want to know what's going on out *there*?"

"Not much to like about *my* world, huh?"

"I'm most concerned with holding on to what I have here."

"So, independence is the main attraction?"

"One, for sure."

"And the others?"

"No cops."

Entry 62: I'm twenty pounds lighter now than when I started this road trip. Beginning to swim in my pants. Need to do some serious shopping at some point soon. Maybe even get a haircut. Been a good four months since it was last cut. Trimming the beard way shorter now. Just stubble, really. The look seems to be in fashion these days, not that it matters to me. I pretty much left that world behind long ago.

Been moving virtually non-stop for so long now and the body's retaliating some, refusing to bounce back each morning as rapidly as it did when I first hit the road. It's clear the wear and tear is taking a slow toll, but not to the point where I'm losing heart. Been thinking about maybe taking a short break to collect my thoughts. A beach somewhere, perhaps. Check into a resort hotel and pamper myself for a couple weeks. Now that I think about it, that's probably not so wise. May get way too comfortable. Lazy. That would be dangerous. No, better to just keep moving. Lots left to see and really not all that much time in which to do it. This country's certainly much broader and more muscled than I thought it would be. I could be on the road for *two* years and still see only a sliver of what's out there.

Entry 63: Woke up in an especially sleazy motel room, even by my standards. Room's cluttered with open bags of chips and cookies. Empty beer cans litter the top of the dresser. A partially drained bottle of *Jose Cuervo* is parked on top of the TV. Ashtray's overflowing with butts. Pieces of crumpled notebook paper are scattered about. On top of all that, my underwear's on backwards and my toothbrush is floating in the toilet. Not good signs.

It was all coming back to me, slowly, but with substantial gaps. I pretty much remember how all this started, just not how it ended.

Stopped off for gas the day before at a speck on the map. Old pumps. No plastic accepted. Had to pay hard cash.

Spotted three teenagers passing around a joint in the vacant lot next to the station. I then did something I never thought I'd ever do again in a million years. I approached them and offered buy some *weed*. Just like that. Straight up. No foreplay. Their jaws dropped and they laughed at me. Can't say I blame them. I'd laugh as well. I produced two twenties and left with a small plastic bag and some paper.

So out of character, but maybe that's *why* I did it. Then again, as fatigue takes root, my defenses are down. There's also a subsurface feeling beginning to bubble up that perhaps all of society's rules just may no longer apply to me. With all my moving about I feel increasingly disconnected from the well-rooted society I see out the car windows. It's almost as if I'm no longer a part of that world and, therefore, not subject to its behavioral expectations.

Drove a few miles out into the desert, down a dirt road going nowhere. Pulled over, rolled one, and fired it up.

Later, fuzzy memories of a *road house.* Crowded. Noisy. Stetson's and boots. Gaudy belt buckles. Buying rounds. Cheers and *high fives.* Karaoke. *"Do You Know the Way to San Jose?"* People laughing, joining in. Stumbling through the *"Texas Two-Step."* Hot breath on my cheek. Cascading hair tickling my nose...

It should be pretty obvious by now to anyone reading this I'm unable to tolerate any stimulate which messes with my head. Even the scent of potpourri has been known to give me a mild buzz.

I understood this limitation long ago and pretty much gave up on anything harder than beer or wine, and then always in carefully monitored moderation. One or two beers or glasses of wine in any twenty-hour period. That was, and is, just about my limit. Any more than that and I run the risk of becoming impossibly charming.

Pretty much everything I know about drugs, and it's not much, was learned from a woman named Tatiana. That was back in the early-seventies right after my marriage fell apart.

Tatiana was a Cuban immigrant, twenty-one, a drug dealer, and drop dead beautiful, the beautiful part all the reason I needed back then to expose myself to the criminal underbelly of Washington, DC.

Between modeling gigs, Tatiana's days and nights were spent trolling for wholesale drugs and then breaking down her buys into small lots, which she sold at a tidy profit on the streets of affluent Georgetown, mostly to congressmen, one senator I recognized, a host of congressional staffers, along with young urban professionals, housewives, high school and college students, their teachers, hippies, restaurateurs, chefs, wait staff, bartenders, doormen, and parking valets, many of the transactions taking place from the passenger seat of my brand new British Racing Green *Triumph GT-6 Mark III* sports car.

When I voiced concern at the prospect of spending years behind bars, Tatiana kept me in line by making sure that night was memorable after the lights were turned off. I was living proof of Napoleon Bonaparte's observation that men are more easily governed through their vices than their virtues.

Tatiana and I didn't last, of course. I was a stiff by comparison to my free-wheeling girlfriend and constantly worried about being busted. My career was on an upward trajectory and I didn't want risk anything which could cause it to come crashing back to earth.

Still, it was a pretty good summer, all things considered.

Took a shower and started straightening up the motel room. Plenty of compelling evidence of overnight company, which I won't get into here. Turn to the crumpled papers. It's my handwriting alright. Try piecing together the scraps. Not totally sure of the order I had in mind when dashing it off, and some of the words are impossible to make out, but this likely comes close:

Old road narrowing. Fading. Doors slammed shut. A generation exiting. Surging through the streets, storming the pillared halls, memories faded and compromised now, and no time, or courage, to reverse (words indecipherable). Hollow alibis replacing substance. Barely glancing back over our shoulders now. Seeing nothing. Feeling less. No white knights. Too many people have died. The retreating sun casts shadows on craggy men and women sitting on porch swings, telling lies to one another. Everything defrocked and fucked over, the spiritual loss of Babylon on the Potomac too terrible to endure. All dust now, little left to salvage, nobility denied, notoriety ensured. No recourse. A shiver. Betrayed. Racing along the cusp of the sensory organs, through lonesome, snow-covered heartland farms. Funneling through fields of bitter melons and withered crops. All the unleashed clarity from a sideline perspective featuring singular verse deposited in mental caverns by unscrupulous purveyors of out-of-tune jukeboxes and generic mindsets fueled by boxed wine. Little left to console but painted hookers with bruised knees, prowling the edges of indifference, a soulless capturing of darkness, all tightly-wound and trembling under thundering hooves passing on floodlit, slippery autobahns of decay. Setting suns, lovers grieving. Survivors shouting mournful dirges from rooftops while licking the rubbery centers of stale Moon Pies. Travel down empty roads, through frozen, barren landscapes hugging the fringes of reality, looking for (words indecipherable) to sleep. Huddling nights in rocky crevices, the wind transporting faint ghostly wails. A seething madhouse. Cultures sucked down sinkholes. Mind awash. Bedeviled. Wrenching. Restless. Haunting moans, intruding. Unholy alliances, rampaging and reneging on promises made at the altar. So many collateral issues defying resolution. Prairie church at noon. Confessed sins but no one's there to listen except an old brown-skin woman sweeping the floor. God is out to lunch. Turn to drink in dives with unruly attitudes. Pausing at a cellar door, drawn by slippery notes from deep inside. Old memories. Half buck burgers and soda fountains, double features and skipping class. Time slipping away. Misspent. Never to be again.

Entry 64: When I pull over for a night, regardless of where I am, there's a way better than fifty-fifty chance the mom-and-pop motel where I lay my head will be owned and run by people from South Asia, primarily India. Talk about an ethic niche.

I can pretty much be in the most remote place in the country, I literally mean the middle of nowhere on the darkest possible night, and be greeted at the front desk at the most modest of motels by a woman in a sari or man in a turban speaking English with a distinct Indo-European accent.

It's taken me a while to get over my surprise at the dominance of South Asians in the motel business, but I've now reached the stage where I'm surprised when the owners of the low-end motels which are my bread and butter on the road are *not* Indian or Pakistani nationals.

"I really like it here in the States," the tall, thin 16-year-old states without hesitation. His name is Pankaj, but asks to be called P.J.

He's been in the country for the past four years and speaks English with just the faintest trace of his native tongue. He's a junior at the small high school, and carries a four-point-o average. Standardized test scores are through the roof.

P.J.'s parents own and operate a twenty-eight unit motel on the north side of the town of five thousand. The motel's not far from the interstate so business is usually pretty good, especially in the summer months when tourists are out and about visiting the nearby national park. Business drags in the wintertime when the snowdrifts are deep, but there's just enough traffic flow to justify staying open year round. The family of six lives in a small, three-bedroom ranch house just behind the motel, the rooms' rich with evidence of spices and aromatics cooking up in the kitchen.

P.J.'s ambition is to attend Stanford with a full academic scholarship. Hopes to be an engineer, or maybe a doctor.

Stanford's quite a leap from this small town, and he knows it better than anyone.

"It hasn't always been easy here, but it's far better than where I was born. Everyone has a place over there and there's little room to maneuver, much less breathe. It's all predetermined. Here, there's no limit to what a person can accomplish...Oh, I was beat up some when I arrived. Called very bad names. Had to fist fight to gain respect. It's pretty much okay now. I have American friends and even play second base on the baseball team, and won a regional high school chess tournament. That meant a lot to the people around here. Lot of pride in achievements in a place this small. Still, some of the adults in town still look at me like I was a bug. I guess they just don't know any better. That attitude has been especially hard on my parents, and even harder on my grandparents. After all this time here, my parents have never been welcomed into an American home. I know that hurts them, and they're lonely, but are accepting of the way it is. The caste system back in my former home is much like that. They didn't have an easy time of it at all back in India, so they still continue to look at America as a land of opportunity. They love it here, although it doesn't love them back."

P.J. is joined by his little sister, Lata, who proudly tells me she recently turned ten. I ask how she likes living here.

"Great!"

"So, what do you want to be when you grow up?"

Lata answers without hesitation. "A cheerleader!"

Entry 65: Not so easy refilling prescriptions out in the wilderness, especially if the medication falls into the rarely prescribed category.

Discovered early on in the road trip it can take two to three days for special deliveries to a small town pharmacy. That's why

I usually wait until I'm in or around a large metropolitan area to put in an order for a new batch of meds, but every once in a while the fact I'm running low slips my mind and I find myself about as far away as the moon from major sources of supply.

I've run into the most problems refilling my heart medication. It's rarely prescribed, very expensive and has a short shelf life. Not something pharmacies would want to keep in stock.

It was in a town in the Mojave Desert when a pharmacist first asked if I were aware just how potent that medicine actually is, and if I knew of the potential side effects.

I pretty much brushed him off by telling him I'd been on the heart drug for years and had not encountered any problems with it. I added I always assumed the cardiologists knew what they were doing, that the meds they prescribed were safe and kept me from meeting a premature end, and I pretty much left it at that.

I stored away my conversation with the rural pharmacist in a place I deposit those subjects I pretty much no longer want to think about. That's the way it was until one night I was watching television in my motel room and a commercial popped-up for some product used to treat an overactive bladder.

I noted a mere fifteen seconds of the minute-long commercial was devoted to actually promoting the benefits of the drug, while the remaining time was taken up warning about the risks. The announcer had to list them in rapid fire order to squeeze them into the time slot.

Drinking grapefruit juice was discouraged, of all things. The same goes for driving a car or operating machinery. It didn't specify what sort of machinery. I suppose I'd have to read the small print to see if a coffee maker or food blender is considered machinery, or if the warning is primarily aimed at bulldozer and backhoe operators.

Turns out this medicine can cause no end of havoc with the immune system, the senses, and everyday bodily functions.

I was surprised the Food and Drug Administration had actually given its stamp of approval to a product which runs the risk of destroying the human body all for the sake of reducing overnight trips to the bathroom.

Against my better judgment, I decide it's time to check out my own medications. I suppose I don't take an inordinate amount of medicine for a man my age. They're four in all. In addition to the heart med, I take a statin to control cholesterol, another pill to keep the blood pressure in check, and *Nexium* each morning to sit on heartburn which may want to bubble to the surface.

Turns out the humble little statin I take each morning can chew up my kidneys and liver, and damage muscle tissue, releasing dangerous proteins into the bloodstream as the muscle tissue is broken down, and all this can eventually lead to fatal complications.

Happily, death wasn't specifically mentioned when it came to my blood pressure medication. The primary side effects include diarrhea, heartburn, dizziness, and fatigue, along with swelling of the neck or head. How does a head swell, by the way? Also thrown into the mix: itching, difficulty swallowing and breathing, sexual problems, angina, hoarseness, changes in the amount of urine produced, chest pain, irregular heartbeat, muscle cramps, and yellowing of the skin or eyes.

The med for controlling acid reflux disease is downright benign by comparison. The worst it could do to me is trigger a headache, diarrhea, and abdominal pain. There's also a risk for bone fractures if taken over an extended period of time. A piece of cake!

I hit the mother lode when it came to my heart medication.

I'm surprised it didn't trigger actual cardiac arrest when I read the cautionary list of possible side effects and realized I suffer from at least five of them, thankfully only moderately, but suffer nonetheless.

In no particular order, the risks include nausea and vomiting, malaise and fatigue, tremors and abnormal involuntary movements, lack of coordination, abnormal gait, dizziness, constipation, anorexia, vision problems, pulmonary inflammation or fibrosis, decreased libido, a tingling, burning, pricking, or numbness of a person's skin, headaches, sleep disturbances, congestive heart failure, liver and kidney damage, flushing, abnormal taste and smell, edema, abnormal salivation, coagulation abnormalities, blue skin discoloration, spontaneous bruising of capillaries, abnormally low blood pressure, and compulsive pulling of hair, which is exactly what I was doing by the time I finished reading the warning label.

Entry 66: Think I've discovered the modern day version of those country stores from another time...places with wood plank floors and sawdust hovering in the air, where locals with craggy, weather-beaten faces, calloused hands, and dressed in dungarees and mud-caked boots, would gather around a potbellied stove on a frosty morning to discuss matters of local interest, from the death of a neighbor's mule to farm subsidies, the price of seed, and the weather. Always the weather!

This shared information would then be disseminated far and wide and the process became critical in the bonding of a rural community back before the widespread availability of telephones and other forms of communication we take for granted today.

Well, the old country store has pretty much vanished from

the American landscape, but there's no underestimating the need people feel to bond with their neighbors.

Today, you'll find people huddled together each morning in, of all places, fast food restaurants. It's a phenomenon that's taken root all across the country. Although meeting at a fast food joint is clearly a step backward in the human evolutionary process, I see it happening everywhere I go. No place is immune. Big city, small town. And all places in-between.

When I spot a gathering, I often try to position myself close enough to these tight-knit clusters of locals to eavesdrop on what's being said...

Man #1: "Y'all see Harold's new pickup yet?"

Man #2: "No, what he buy himself?"

Man #1: "A *Ford*. A used one. One of them big numbers. Three tons or better. Drove over around supper yesterday to let Babs and me take a look at it. Real nice. Sure wish I had one myself, but there's a lot of things I can say that about."

Man #2: "Amen to that!"

Man #3: "Heard Harold had to bring in his sister-in-law from over in Lewiston to help out with things since Martha fell sick again."

Man#4: "I suppose she's having that same old problem?"

Man #3: "Yeah. Damn shame that is. Been going on for quite a while now."

Man #4: "It looks pretty bad, although she still manages to smile that smile. Martha's smile could always lighten up a dark day."

Man #5: "I tell you health's all we got in this world that's worth anything."

Man #2: "Amen to that!"

Man #3 (annoyed): "You know Willie, you're always saying

amen, but you never go to church. Never been as long as I can remember and that's a good forty years. You didn't even get married in church."

Man #2 (grinning): "Then what you suggest I say? *Amen* sounds better than *fucking-A*."

Man #5 (laughing): "He's got you there, Fred."

Man #4: "Speaking of health, forget to tell you Larry Crenshaw's been told he's got prostate cancer. Doc Wilson's nurse let it slip when talking to Carrie on the phone last night. Told Carrie not to spread it around, but good luck with that. You know how women talk. The good news is the cancer doesn't appear to be too advanced. They seem to have caught it in time. 'Course he'll likely be laid up for a while, or at the very least be forced to cut back on work during treatment. Lucky he's got those three boys to help out around the place."

Man #3: "Only two right now, actually. Billy's still in prison."

Man #2: "I thought I heard he was paroled."

Man #3: "Everyone was expecting it, but he got turned down for doing some shit. Got another eighteen months to serve out now. Least ways that's what I heard."

Man #5: "Something was never quite right about that boy. That's just how it can be with people, you know. They're born that way and there's nothing can be done about it. He tried to date my Jenny once. Asked her to some dance over at the V.F.W. I put a stop to that fast enough, even though Jenny put up a big fuss. I had a bad feeling about him, even back then. Easy to see the direction he was heading would lead to no good."

Man #4: "Kid takes some after his old man, at least when he was young. Crenshaw was one tough customer before he calmed down during that stint in the Army. A whole different man, that's for sure. Something must have happened to him there, but he never talks about it and I ain't about to ask what it was."

Man #5: "You sure as hell didn't want to mess around none with him when he was a youngster. Saw him pound the piss out of the Waller twins one Labor Day picnic. They were bothering his kid sister so he walked right over and gave it to them, right there in front of everyone. Sheriff's deputies looked the other way. Guess they figured the twins deserved an ass-whippin' as well."

Man #5: "Say, any of you hear the people who bought the Morrison spread are planning to raise alpaca?"

Man #5: "What the hell's an *al-whatyousay*?"

Man #4: "Alpaca. It's an animal."

Man #5: "I sure never heard of it. What they look like?"

Man #4: "Saw one the other day in a horse trailer parked in town. Strange looking critter. Big thing, has a really long neck, pointy ears, and is furry."

Man #5: "Where they come from?"

Man #4: "Don't know. Someplace foreign, for sure. Maybe China, or could be Africa. Some place like that."

Man #5: "What they good for anyway? Eating?"

Man #4: "I really don't know. They sure don't look they'd taste much good, but I guess you could say the same thing about squirrels, pigs and stuff till you learned better."

Man #5: "Why would someone want to go and do something like that for? Cattle's been good enough around here forever, and I see no reason for that to change. No telling what new type livestock will do to the grazing lands. They're barely hanging on as it is."

Man: #1: "I don't understand the world sometimes. Moving way too fast for my liking. Sometimes seems the old ways are not good enough no more."

A tall, silver-haired woman in a chartreuse pant suit enters the restaurant. The men hoot and wave and she walks over, smiling broadly and working the hell out of a stick of gum.

Woman: “Hey there, boys. See you’re busy as usual doing important stuff. Your wives know what you’re up to?”

Man #3: “You’re looking mighty fine, Becky. As good as you did in high school, for sure. Maybe better, if that’s possible.”

Woman (smiling, enjoying the compliment): “High school?! You can remember that far back, can ya?”

Man #3: “Hard to forget someone as pretty as you were. That kind of sticks with a fella. Can’t shake that off so easy.”

Woman: “You always were a sweet talker. Full of it, but a sweet talking man, that’s for sure. I’m surprised we never slept together back then.”

Man #3: “You’re kidding me, right?! We went steady for nearly a whole year. Everybody knows that.”

Woman (smiling): “Funny, I don’t remember that at all. I guess sleeping with you wasn’t all that memorable.”

Entry 67: Can’t tell you how many times I’m asked out on the road where I’m from. It’s a totally logical and inoffensive icebreaker when meeting strangers, and ranks right up there with our name and what we do as the most common questions we ask of one another.

For most people, the name of their hometown just rolls off the tongue without a moment’s hesitation. For me, it’s not so easy to answer. I often say North Carolina, but am equally liable to answer Washington, DC. I’m sometimes tempted to say my home is where I hang my hat that particular evening, but that would just label me as eccentric, and I get enough of that already without adding fuel to the fire.

I suppose if I *had* to choose somewhere to call home, it would be a place which no longer really exists, except in my memory.

To get there requires leaving *U.S. One* behind at *Cranes Creek Road,* crossing over the railroad tracks, traveling up the narrow lane and, at the spot where it bends to the left, there's a tall stand of oak and pine trees and, in the spring, great flowing tentacles and thick knots of wisteria, and a towering magnolia tree in full bloom which stood witness to the ebb and flow of life on the Thompson family farm.

The farmhouse is gone now, a victim of time, indifference, and bulldozers clearing the way for the *Highway One Bypass.* About all that's left there is a clearing covered with ground vines, barely discernible outlines of age-old sandy footpaths, a chunk of a chimney, a well cover, and other bits and pieces scattered around.

My father was born there, and his father, and his father's father.

The land is rich with Thompson blood, sweat, joy, hope, and heartache. It took a century and a half to build, one generation to bring it down. No secret why. The land grew tired; the people grew tired and drifted away. Urbanization, the lure of the big city, and the demise of the small family farm forever sealed the fate of the place.

Walking over the now abandoned land makes me feel somewhat diminished as a person, questioning of "progress," and sensitive to our limited time and lingering impact. One thing, however, which can't be bulldozed under are my memories from the nineteen-fifties of a city kid who had the good fortune from time to time to spend seemingly endless summer days on the farm, riding bareback on mules, feeling the hot Carolina sand between my toes, tugging on my grandfather's handlebar mustache, swimming in the muddy creek as my dad held vigil on the bank, a .22-rifle at his side should a water moccasin slither too close.

A big treat was walking down the dusty road to Routh's Filling Station for a *Coca-Cola* plucked from the icy innards of a huge lift-top insulated chest located under a tin awning which also shaded the early hand-cranked gas pump. If I had an extra nickel, I'd snap up a *Baby Ruth or Zagnut* from the sweets rack inside nestled between rough-hewn barrels of seed, nails, and rock hard soda crackers. To this very day, I can still feel that ice cold, sweaty soda bottle in my hands and the shiver it sent through me when I rubbed it against my cheek on a blistering hot August afternoon.

The kitchen was by far my favorite room in the farmhouse. Aunt Glennie always seemed to be there, rolling and baking endless trays of biscuits, shucking corn and plucking chickens for supper, all the while working on a pinch of snuff, the juicy residue she'd deposit in an old coffee can.

We all ate together at a long wood table dark and rich with the patina from the touch of generations of family.

Prayer first, then "pass the biscuits!"

The first Thompson reached the county in the year eighteen twenty on the back of a gray mule.

My great-great grandfather Jesse was a farmer, but on weekends rode off to preach the gospel. My great grandfather Bryant inherited the land and somehow managed to hold onto it through war, drought, and economic downturns. The land dominated every thought and action of the early Thompson's. After all, it was the mortar which bonded and sustained the family unit.

Bryant walked away from the Confederate Army one early spring when no menfolk were left to work the farm. Family historians say he put on the dress and bonnet of his bride to work undetected in the fields, and one evening actually hid in the chimney when an army patrol came looking for him.

He returned to duty when the crops were growing strong and went on to survive the Battle of Gettysburg.

The Civil War left the men and women of the Cranes Creek community bitter, disillusioned and destitute. While dutifully marching off to battle, the Thompson clan almost universally considered the War Between the States a threat to what little they had in life.

Isaac, a great-great uncle stationed with the North Carolina 46th Infantry Regiment in Richmond, wrote to a friend that if the war dragged on much longer "*starvation will visit the land with great destruction, and if my family has to suffer and die for want of something to eat, what good would it do for me to gain independence?*"

As a boy sitting on the farmhouse porch in the cool of the evening at the feet of old men, the debate on the war still raged on with much passion ninety years after it drew to a close. I can still hear my grandfather telling everyone with great conviction the South didn't lose the war to better fighting men. "We lost," he said, "because we got plum wore out beating the Yankees in battle after battle in the early part of the war."

My father was born on the farm in the autumn of nineteen twelve, the next to youngest of nine children of Edward Braxton Thompson and Newell Elizabeth McDuffie, a saintly, six foot tall woman who'd taught in one room school houses across the Sandhills.

Times were brutal back then, money virtually non-existent. My father slept in pajamas his mother sewed out of flour sacks. When salt was in short supply, Bryant devised a method to extract it from the smokehouse floor. Teeth were pulled the old fashioned way—with household pliers. My father's tonsils were removed as he was tied down in a barber's chair. My great grandma "Lizzie" was the community nurse and made her own remedies for ailing neighbors from wines, herbs, and fox grapes.

The farmhouse had no running water, no electricity. Fireplaces and a wood stove provided the heat. In winter, people slept three to four to a bed huddled close under mounds of hand-made down quilts. An outhouse stood alongside a narrow path out the side door, an adventure to reach on an icy dawn, or endure when the summer sun cooked the land. It was nearly nineteen fifty before electricity and telephone service reached the farm.

Grandpa, a short, wiry, taciturn man with piercing blue eyes, was a farmer and carpenter by trade, but made time to serve as Town Marshal, and each Sunday morning made sure his brood made it to church, traveling together in a wagon pulled by a mule named either Jack, Maude or Nell.

From this man the children learned to respect the land and hard work. From their mother came a love of the written word. In the evening after supper, the children would gather around my grandmother by the fireplace in the parlor where she would read from the classics, Shakespeare, North Carolina poets, and the Bible. She passed away just a few weeks before I was born, not so old in years, but wasted in body. Grandpa lived to nearly ninety.

From the children gathered around that fireplace on that desperately poor, isolated farm in the heart of *Tobacco Road*, would soon emerge a diplomat, minister, attorney, merchants, educators, and healers, all of whom were fiercely determined from a young age to escape the chronic poverty and hardship. It was this sudden exodus by virtually an entire generation which ultimately sealed the fate of the family farm.

They're all gone now, everyone, but I can still visit many of them at the Johnson Grove Cemetery over in Vass. They lie close together under towering pines on what is the last surviving piece of land in the county a Thompson from Cranes Creek Road can still call home.

Entry 68: Sunday morning. The parking lot to the *First Congregational Church* across the street from the motel is filling up fast. For a fleeting moment, I actually consider attending the service. Can't do any harm, and maybe even do some good, I reason, and then I drop the thought entirely.

God and I have never had much of a relationship, as far as I can tell, although He may have been out there watching over me when I needed watching, which was often. I do believe in a higher force or structure of some kind directing traffic here on earth, and the universe, but I've probably seen far too much to embrace religion in the conventional sense.

For some people, witnessing the darkest side of the human race drives them closer to God. It hasn't worked out that way for me, although I do like to keep my options open for a dramatic transformation at some point down the road. For now, let's just say I wobble between the two worlds.

These days I've been known to darken the door of a church for weddings and funerals, other times on Christmas Eve for the music, and at Easter if I happen to be romantically involved with a Catholic who absolutely insists on my accompanying her to Mass.

My all-time favorite joke certainly doesn't bode well for helping grease the way into the abode of angels.

Jesus is on the cross. His followers are nearby, praying and weeping. Jesus calls out to one of them. "Peter, Peter." Peter frantically pushes his way through the throng and the Roman guards ringing the base of the cross. "I'm coming

Master, I'm coming!" Roman guards tackle and punish Peter by chopping off his arms, and then throw him back into the wailing crowd. Jesus calls out again. Peter stumbles back to the cross. This time the Romans lop off Peters legs. Jesus persists. "Peter, Peter." Peter wiggles through the legs of the Romans and looks up at Jesus. "I'm here, I'm here!" Jesus speaks: "Peter, I can see your house from up here."

I've had my fair share of encounters with religious heavyweights over the years, thanks to my profession.

For example, there's the time Pope John-Paul visited South Korea and it fell to me to cover the event. I wasn't happy with the assignment. Security would be brutal, the crowds massive, sleep elusive, and I knew next to nothing of papal rituals, etiquette, and teachings, and wasn't all that anxious to learn.

The Pope's busy schedule called for a visit one morning to an island of lepers, and I was among the handful of reporters selected for *pool coverage* of the event, meaning when we returned to the mainland, it would be our responsibility to brief reporters left behind on what happened.

Let me set the scene:

John-Paul is about to enter a small chapel where he'll actually lay his hands on suffering lepers. Clutching a microphone, I take up a choice position with camera crews near the door through which we've been alerted he'll make his grand entrance. No sooner than we settle in, the door swings open and there stands John-Paul not three feet away, decked out in his normal day-to-day white dress and skullcap. A large gold cross hangs around his neck.

The Pontiff's face is serene, gentle and kind, just as he always appears in photographs and on television. That abruptly changes, however, the moment John-Paul catches sight of me.

He looks directly into my eyes and stops dead in his tracks, his face betraying actual fear. The look is there but for a second or two, but it's clearly there. The Pope then breaks eye contact, takes a deep breath, and quickly brushes past me, so close I can feel the air stirred by his passing body.

Understandably, that brief encounter has stuck with me through the years. I've often asked myself what could have possibly filled John-Paul with such dread. The most logical answer I could come up with—the one with the fewest complications—was some three years earlier the Pope had taken assassins bullets in St. Peter's Square, fired by a young bearded man with long hair. I rationalized that since I also had a beard, longish hair, was pointing a metal object (the microphone) at him, and was literally in his face when the door opened, his Holiness sensed he was in trouble and froze. Seems a normal enough human reaction given the trauma of what happened at the Vatican.

Then again, maybe that explanation is *too* convenient. What if in his papal wisdom John-Paul saw something else, something dark and sinister lurking in my soul, something which chilled him to the bone?

That worried me for a long time. Still does every now and then. After all, it's not so easy brushing aside the memory of scaring the *bejesus* out of a future saint and the spiritual leader of one billion souls.

Many years later.

I'm in a bathroom at the Washington headquarters taking a break after a long recording session for some public service show.

I'd no sooner taken up position at a urinal when someone slides into the one next to mine. I look over at the man. It's just a short, side glance, mind you. A kind of reflex action.

Protracted staring at other men in public bathrooms is unwise, but something about *this* man makes me take a second look.

This time he's looking back at me, and smiling. It takes a second to register, but when it does it strikes with a thunderous clap and may have resulted in some errant spray around my urinal.

I'm in the presence of ... the Dalai Lama!

No question about it. No one else looks quite the same. Short, bald guy, glasses, wears funny-looking clothing, exudes kindness, goodness, and all that other important stuff which goes with the job.

I'd heard he was in town for a series of interviews, fund-raising events, and a meeting with the President at the White House, and here he was taking a leak in my presence.

The Dalai Lama and I exchange quick nods and return to the business at *hand.*

I recall wondering how he managed to stand and relieve himself with that robe wrapped around him like that. I thought a sitting position made more sense, but looked over my shoulder and noticed the three stalls had been roped off for repairs of some kind. I decided against sneaking a peek around the low barrier between us to find out how the Dalai Lama is getting the job done. Some things are just better left unexplored.

Anyway, we finish at the same time and find ourselves washing hands in side-by-side sinks. The Dalai Lama imparts no profound words of wisdom which compel me to launch a global mission to try to set right all the ills of the world. He merely tells me how much he likes American bathrooms. He's especially fond of those push-button hand soap dispensers, and prefers paper hand towels over roaring electric dryers.

I'm tempted to take the conversation into more lofty realms when one of his aides appears in the doorway. It's time to go.

The Dalai Lama and I exchange quick goodbyes and go our separate ways...he to enlightening mankind, and me to lunch at *Wendy's*.

Entry 69: I've decided to take a break and scoot back to North Carolina to spend Christmas at my son's home near Raleigh. Can't bear the thought of the holidays alone in a fleabag motel, so I'll torture myself with what amounts to a six thousand mile roundtrip.

While back there, I may as well get my annual physical exam out of the way, see a dentist and, as I head back to the West Coast, take the route through to the Deep South so I can visit my daughters and grandkids.

But before I shut down the journal for a while, there's a Christmas story I'd like to share with you this joyous holiday season.

Living overseas at Christmas always proved a challenge... finding a proper tree, lights for it, ornaments, gift-wrapping, mistletoe, a Butterball Turkey...You get the general idea. It was also not so easy being embraced by the *Christmas spirit* due to a dearth of everyday holiday reminders...which leads to my little story.

Many years ago, the management of a major department store in Tokyo decided to explore, and hopefully exploit, the commercial possibilities of Christmas. Lots of westerners with fat wallets lived there, and maybe the local populace could even be enticed to join in the gift-buying frenzy. The potential for a financial windfall was enormous. The Japanese, after all, loved all things Western so it was not a far-fetched idea.

The decision was made to create a festive Christmas scene in the nearly half block long storefront window to try to lure shoppers into the store where a mirthful Christmas department would be created and well-stocked with pricey items.

Management and the window decorators worked hard to bring together in a contained space all the assorted elements of the Christmas season. Wasn't an easy undertaking. After all, this was Shinto-land and Christianity never had all that much of a foothold in Japan, so no one was totally clear on how all the holiday pieces should exactly fit together.

The grand unveiling of the window proved to be a media event. The window was certainly festive. There was a painted Currier & Ives wintery backdrop featuring children skating on an ice pond, a horse-drawn sleigh, and carolers out in the snow. The centerpiece of the window display was a huge Christmas tree bristling with lights and ornaments. Gaily-wrapped gifts were under that tree, stockings were hung by the chimney with care. There was also a red-nosed reindeer, a nativity scene, the Star of Bethlehem dangling from the ceiling, and then there was jolly old Santa Claus...nailed to a cross.

-IV-

The Road Trip Journal, Part Two

Entry 70: Reach the Monterrey Peninsula just in time to catch the sun sliding onto the Pacific.

Take a quick look around town before it gets dark. Must say Monterey's impressive. A beautiful, cultured community of theaters and museums, *Cannery Row*, and adobe buildings which have stood for two centuries. John Steinbeck's from around here, and Henry Miller and Robert Lewis Stevenson lived and worked in town. Painters, too. Mathews, Hansen, and Meeks, to name a few. Clint Eastwood and Doris Day live in the neighborhood. *Play Misty for Me* was filmed here, along with the famous kiss Burt Lancaster and Deborah Kerr shared in that iconic beach scene in *From Here to Eternity*.

It's been a demanding, no frills, cross-country drive and my body's in full rebellion right now. Sleep's coming hard at me. Will surrender to it. Big day tomorrow so want to be fresh.

Entry 71: The primary reason I drove all the way to the Pacific Ocean was to take in the spectacular scenery in the Big Sur region, which runs for some one hundred miles along the legendary *Highway One* coastal roadway.

To my dismay, landslides have shut down a long stretch of the road cutting through, of course, the most dramatic, desirable sections. I pound the steering wheel in frustration and head straight for the village of Carmel-by-the-Sea to console myself with an impossibly expensive, butter-laden lunch.

Fail to catch-sight of Clint, who was town mayor around here at one time. Easy to see why he chose to settle here. This is a storybook community. Just flawless. The streets are narrow and tree-lined, the taverns, bistros, galleries, and boutiques top shelf, picture perfect cottages and chalets line the side streets. There are no parking meters here, no numbered addresses, or even street lamps, and the rocky coastline is but a few steps from the village center, the beach trimmed in cypress trees, twisted into ghostly shapes by the indefatigable sea breeze.

My lunch is "real" food, cooked in a "real" kitchen, by someone who actually knows what they're doing. A wonderful change of pace from my normal fare. Well worth the forty dollar tab, but this means I'll be eating beans for the next few days. Damn budget is getting on my nerves, but I can't blink now, not this far along in my journey.

Hate to leave this village but I have a ways to travel before I can call it a day. Timetable's been thrown out of whack by the road closure, so I need to get moving. No choice now but to set out on an inland route to reach my next coastal destination, Morro Bay, at the southern end of Big Sur.

The meandering detour takes me through Salinas Valley, the so-called "Salad Bowl to the World." Never have I seen such agricultural activity. Fields stretching forever, great chains of workers bent over picking and planting, long caravans of trucks being loaded and sent on their way. I'll never be able to look at a *Chef's Salad* the same way again.

Must say I'm more than a little surprised at the overall seediness of the area. No palpable sense of vitality in the string of weary little towns I pass through. Not what you'd expect given the lushness and bounty of the harvest. Revenue generated by the agricultural bonanza certainly doesn't appear to be plowed back into the local economy, at least in any meaningful way that's obvious to me. There are jobs to be had, yes, but something deeper is missing from the equation. Just possibly a soul.

Steinbeck captured the flavor decades ago. He worked these very fields as a young man and drew inspiration from what he saw here for characters he created for *The Grapes of Wrath* and *East of Eden*.

Once the Valley's cleared, I head back towards the coast and reach Morro Bay at dinnertime. Motel website promised oceanfront. I have oceanfront alright, but to get there requires crossing a high-speed four lane highway, scaling two fences, and covering two hundred yards of mud flats.

This has clearly not been the best of days. Even the rich lunch lies heavy in my stomach.

Entry 72: I'm up and out the door at five this morning to explore the southernmost reaches of the road leading up to Big Sur. Don't get very far. More landslides. Road barricaded. What gives with California, anyway?! Not much in the way of scenery to speak of, I'm afraid, and the fog rolling down the sheer cliffs makes driving along the twisting, narrow mountain road a miserable experience.

Happily, the day's not a total washout. When I pull over to snap a few photos of the Pacific as the fog burns off, the ground beneath my feet absolutely trembles from guttural trumpeting sounds. I look down a hill to the beach and spread out on the sand among the rocks are several hundred massive, blubbery female elephant seals, huddled close, some sound asleep, others competing for space. There's a lot of pushing and shoving and half-hearted biting and head-butting.

Ignoring the signs planted about instructing people to steer clear of face-to-face encounters with the ponderous, ill-mannered beasts, I climb down a hill to the sand for a better look and to snap some up-close photos.

Quickly discover the high ground is the preferable place to be in the presence of these unruly creatures. An elephant seal is fast on her *fins*, and I'm not as fast as I once was, not by a longshot. A female of copious girth charges. My churning legs are kicking up sand but I not going anywhere. In the nick of time I catch some traction and scamper back up the hill. The twelve-foot long, fifteen hundred pound cow stops and follows my escape, bellows in triumph, then flops to the sand and is soon fast asleep.

Entry 73: Had been planning to hang around here for a few weeks, but decide to pull up stakes and hit the road. Without Big Sur not much else around is of equal interest. Besides, the town's overrun with tourists, and prices are on the high side.

Want to head over to magnificent Yosemite where Ansel Adams did his legendary, ground-breaking photography, but learn the main road slicing through the park is closed thanks to snow, packed ice, fallen trees, landslides, and avalanches. It's clear I'm not having much luck with California. Guess I'll head out in the morning, drive inland for a bit and then slowly drift in a northerly direction and see what crosses my path.

Entry 74: Driving along a two-lane road cradled between a pair of burnished hills, with a commanding view of the distant Pacific Ocean, I spot an avocado orchard off to my right—a rolling hillside blanketed with the dark green, leafy trees packed tightly together in neat rows.

Never been around an avocado tree before so decide to take

a closer look. Pull into an open gate and spot a woman holding a clipboard standing beside a *Range Rover.* Ask if it would be okay to take my camera out among the heavily-laden trees for a few minutes. She surprises by taking me on a personal tour.

This is one attractive woman. A contemporary. Slender, short silver hair, the palest of blue eyes, and impossibly high cheekbones. She's wearing khaki slacks and a dark green safari shirt with the sleeves rolled up.

We stroll along paths cutting through the orchard, stopping several times as she parcels out instructions to workers tending the trees. She explains to me in detail the lifecycle of an avocado, how it matures on the tree, ripens on the ground, when and how to ship it to market. Easy to see the genuine love for what's she doing.

She walks tall and confident, and is easy to like. She pulls me in instantly. No drama to any of it. Barriers erode. Old ghosts stir. I'll concern myself later with potential complications, but the moment is now and I want to enjoy it.

I ask her name. It's Eve.

She picks up an avocado, expertly opens it with a pocket knife, digs a finger into the warm, soft, creamy flesh...and holds it up to my lips.

Entry 75: Eve takes me to her favorite restaurant for dinner. A dockside seafood place with a restful sunset view. We both order sea bass. The wine is local.

A long time ago, in a far different world, Eve was a *hippie,* although she laughs when she says she prefers the term "enlightened anarchist." Did the Berkeley counterculture scene in the nineteen sixties and was jailed briefly several times as revolution swept the campus. Moved up the coast to Height-Ashbury. Wore flowers in her hair. Experimented with drugs and free love. Shared a walk-up flat for a while with Janis Joplin. Got to know Jerry Garcia. Painted. Wrote poetry. Distributed food to the *street people.* Moved on when Height-Ashbury became too "mainstream." Married a hippy turned organic farmer. No children. Miscarried three times. Widowed two years earlier, and took over the day-to-day running of the one hundred five acre orchard.

Entry 76: Sunday. Eve and I explore the rocky coastline to the south. Stop for a picnic lunch at the edge of a cliff overlooking a vast expanse of rolling, white-capped ocean. Pull over later along an especially breathtaking stretch of coastal road. Pay our respects to the ghosts of the early writers and artists drawn to this isolated natural beauty to escape the air conditioned madness of life inland. I'm feeling good, really good. Revitalized.

Entry 77: Move out of the motel and in with Eve. A pretty beach cottage on a stretch of rocky shore. I'm determined to learn all there is about her, subjects which hadn't come up in our first week together—like whether she's allergic to peanuts and likes Gershwin, knows the lyrics to *Da Do Ron Ron,* and has ever been to Spain...

Entry 78: Several weeks since the last entry. Time passing so effortlessly. The soil, the sea, one another, and little room for much else, and we wouldn't have it any other way.

Entry 79: Our end-of-day ritual is to curl up in a blanket on the porch swing with a glass of wine and gaze out to sea. No words are necessary. Nature lays out more than enough before us on her banquet table to make speech superfluous...waves lapping against the *sea stacks* rising from the deep; gulls momentarily silhouetted against the last surviving sigh of the long vanished sun; a pod of dolphins navigating a watery road home; the budding stars, as vivid as diamonds strewn on black velvet; a lighthouse casting its beam across the vastness; an unknown power speaking through the thunderheads building inland...

-V-

Turning the Corner

Entry 80: First entry in days. Up at dawn, standing on a rocky cliff scanning the churning Pacific through sheets of cold rain, hoping to catch a glimpse of a migrating gray whale, but see nary a splash, vapor puff, or tail fluke. My sole company's a few hearty seagulls battling strong headwinds, and the distant Battery Point Lighthouse, which has stood guard over the harbor for more than a century and a half.

Don't feel like writing, or pretty much anything else for that matter. Road trip's on an entirely new path now. Impossible not to linger on what was, what might have been, and what *still* could be. Old habits intruded. That much is clear. Can't fully explain it and I don't even want to try, at least not now, and certainly not here. Eve told me she understands. Taking some comfort in that. Miss her, of course, but I have promises to keep...and I am who I am. Not at all pleased with myself right now, and that's all I'm going to say on the matter.

In far northern California, in an oceanfront town a few miles from the Oregon state line. I'm here for the nearby giant Redwoods. Setting out for the groves at first light.

Entry 81: Not sure what I expected when mapping out a visit to the Redwood Forests. Oh, I knew the trees were huge and old, but not much else. I certainly didn't expect the ancients to cast such a spell on me.

I start down a narrow trail cutting through a thick stand of trees draped in early morning mist. Astonishingly beautiful. So quiet and still. I can't escape the feeling I'm standing in nature's version of the Sistine Chapel. All that's missing is a rush of soaring choral music to punctuate the moment.

I slowly approach an especially imposing specimen. Not easy catching my breath when I consider this giant stood here during the fall of the Roman Empire, the Dark Ages, and the Renaissance. It was already *very* old when Columbus set sail and the Pilgrims landed in the *New World*. There's a strong probability it was even around when Jesus walked the earth. Two thousand years. Imagine that.

The redwood stands at least three hundred feet in height and it takes better than two minutes to navigate my way around the gnarled and knotted base, heavy with a confusion of vegetation. The tree's limbless for the first one hundred fifty feet or so then branches start appearing. The battered bark's two feet thick at the base and blackened from centuries of lightning strikes and forest fires. This is one tough customer.

I want to photograph this redwood, but am stymied. It's simply too massive for my lens to capture, literally and otherwise. I surrender, put the camera back into its carrying case, and take a seat on an imposing root, one of many radiating from the redwood base across the perpetually-wet forest floor ruled by dripping Jurassic ferns.

The tree tapers upward, vanishing into a leafy darkness. I crane my neck but am unable to see the sky. No bright sunlight here. Not even close. Just a trickle of light is allowed to filter down to the surface. God only knows what nights here are like. Not sure I'd want to experience that.

It begins to rain. A drizzle at first, then heavier. I walk deeper into the grove and find myself standing in a gathering of redwood saplings. Tiny for now, twig-like and vulnerable, giving no hint at what's to come, but doubtless all eager for their turn to stretch skyward to join the soaring majesty which has fogged the very definition of time.

Entry 82: The bright sun is full of promise, but the straight-line wind carries a sullen chill which erodes any benefit the sunshine may offer.

Clearly spring is slow to come to the highlands of Oregon this year, but I don't have to tell that to the residents of this backwoods hamlet where I've stopped for lunch and gas. They know that well enough, even though they're walking around in their summer clothes despite the fact the temperature is hovering at the freezing mark and mountains of plowed snow frame the main street through town.

The woman who pumps my gas (*self-service* at the gas pump is illegal in Oregon) tells me everyone's dressed this way because they're trying to make it perfectly clear to winter that it's stayed beyond its time and should clear out to make room for the season of renewal impatiently waiting in the wings.

"Enough of this bitching cold!" she shouts into the obstinate wind. "It's been a really hard winter and everyone's fed up. By now it should be at least fifty, not twenty! Tempers around here are growing short, especially mine, as you can probably tell."

The young woman clears her throat and lowers the decibel level. "By the way, in case you were wondering, it's okay to tip me if you like. Out-of-staters like yourself from places where you do your own pumping are never certain what to do about that, so I like to set them straight right away. They seem to appreciate it. Makes the experience less awkward, if you know what I mean. People are under no obligation to tip, of course, but most do. A dollar usually does it, although some people have dropped a fiver on me. Guy once gave me a twenty, but he was from New York City and probably nuts anyway."

She's dressed in a sleeveless *Seahawks* sweatshirt, cut-off jeans, and moccasins. Her exposed skin is deep pink and freckled with goose bumps. I, on the other hand, expose little flesh thanks to careful layering up. A sweater hides under a wool pee coat. I'm wearing boots and insulated socks, along with corduroy trousers. Gloves and scarf complete the winter outfit.

I'm not sure which of us looks the most ridiculous—me or the half-dressed woman pumping gas in numbing weather. Probably me. After all, I'm the non-conformist in these parts.

I tip her two bucks.

Entry 83: As I enter the eastern reaches of Oregon, closing in on Idaho, the land takes on a whole new look. I'd always considered *all* of Oregon to be a lush garden and am surprised to see such a quick transformation to an arid, barren one, almost desert-like.

At the same time, there are pearls to be found in small, protected valleys rich with picturesque lakes, rivers and streams, blooming cottonwood trees, greening pastures, and grazing sheep and cattle. I never cease being amazed at what nature keeps throwing my way day after day. I can't stop smiling.

Entry 84: The snow remains deep in Wyoming's Tetons. The highest peaks, reaching upwards of fourteen thousand feet, are blanketed in a wintery display which extends all the way down to the Jackson Hole Valley floor.

I pretty much have the Grand Teton National Park all to myself this morning. The reason for that could be the single digit wind chill factor, towering snowdrifts, slick roads, frozen lakes, and brooding open range.

Resumed my moose *hunt* again today. Been going after a photograph for a long time now, but moose are shy and ghostly creatures. Oh, I'll spot them from time to time silhouetted against the mountains, but the creatures melt back into the landscape before I can get close enough for even my telephoto lens to do much good. When I'd just about given up hope, my luck turns.

Spotted her grazing not one hundred yards off the gravel road. I leave the car and set out on foot, slowly cutting the distance between us through a series of right angle tacks and not a head-on approach which would surely spook her.

The winter's clearly been tough on the old gal. She's scrawny and wobbly on her legs, her weather-beaten coat devoid of great patches of hair along her flanks, hind quarters and undercarriage. A long, matted beard hangs from her neck. If she were human, I'd describe the look on her face as forlorn and resigned.

Cozy up to her as she grazes on a bush, careful to keep at least some kind of vegetation between the two of us in case she decides to charge. But she pretty much ignores me, lacking either the will, or energy, to object to my presence, even when I foolishly abandon all caution and reach out and stroke her back. She just looks at me with those sad eyes, snorts once, and returns to her meal.

Entry 85: Twenty-two degrees and the wind's a sandblaster when I pull out of the parking lot of the *Pony Express Motel* in Jackson, on a day trip to Yellowstone.

The weather may be appalling but since I'm already this close I can't very well pass up an opportunity to check out the so-called *"crown jewel"* of the park system. I'd timed my arrival in the Tetons with the arrival of spring, but these mountains have their own way of measuring time.

It's an easy enough thirty-minute drive from the town of Jackson to the park's South Gate, but when I reach there the ranger on duty informs me the entrance is closed to traffic. It seems fifteen feet of snow blanketing the road has yet to be plowed. Fifteen feet!

He offers me an alternative, if I'm up to it. I can still get to see Yellowstone provided I'm willing to drive up to the now open West Gate. It won't be an easy drive. Two hours or more, he cautions, but if I'm determined to see Yellowstone today, or anytime soon, I really have no other choice. I decide to go for it.

The ranger draws me a map. I'll have to head due west for Idaho, drive north along a stretch of suspect back roads, cross over into Montana and enter Yellowstone from there. A drive of some one hundred miles.

The route's easy enough at first. Other than a few patches of icy pavement on hairpin roads to watch out for, I make good time. The situation changes halfway there when *"Travel at Your Own Risk"* signs start showing up on frost-heaved and black-iced country roads. The signs warn in clear enough English if I become stranded out here, I'm pretty much on my own.

I'm somewhat comforted I'd brought along a *Thermos* of hot tea, water, and a blanket. I calculate I could probably survive fifteen, eighteen hours entombed in a snow bank before dying of exposure. Some comfort.

Reach the tourist town of West Yellowstone at mid-morning. Not a soul around, which isn't surprising given the conditions. This is a summer town and I have a feeling conditions which most people normally associate with spring—flowers, green lawns, leaves on trees, and such—do not take hold here until late-June, if then. I'm not happy with myself for miscalculating so badly.

I head straight for the park entrance. As it is I only have a short time to visit before I need to start heading back to Jackson along the same torturous route I drove to get here. Darkness falls early and I don't want to be out on those roads after dark.

Yellowstone's beautiful, of course, at least the small section I'm able to see in a few hurried hours. The wildlife's abundant, the steaming geysers remarkable, the land pristine. No manmade sounds out here. Just the whistling, unstoppable wind, the howl of a deep woods wolf, and a wedge of trumpeting geese following the path of the river cutting through the valley. Spot a pair of coyotes racing across a ridgeline, ears pinned back, eyes fixed straight ahead. Just visible over the massive snow bank lining the side of the road, a score of ice-coated buffalo trudging across a lifeless field. Steam billows skyward as overheated water in the cauldron of underground volcanic activity spews forth from hundreds of geysers and collides with the frozen air...

The sun's well along in its downward trajectory when a light snow arrives on a bitter wind. I look at my watch. It's time to go.

Entry 86: Next day. Attempt to drive north out of Jackson, but the snow's coming down with a vengeance.

Had hoped to reach the Little Big Horn by sundown, but the road narrows and grows more treacherous the farther I drive, eventually disappearing from view entirely beneath a white sheet. No choice but to retreat thirty miles back to Jackson, and then continue on south. So much for seeing where Custer made his *last stand.*

Snow stalks my bumper for the next six hours. Manage to keep one step ahead of it most of the way, but there are unsettling compacts of time when it wraps in tight around me, obliterating the horizon and enveloping me in a world of white where no shadows are cast. But I continue to plow ahead, and am eventually rewarded with the return of the earth and sky.

Weather improves considerably by the time I reach Laramie, Wyoming.

Laramie was founded some one hundred fifty years earlier as a tent city along the *Overland Stage Line* route and the *Union Pacific* portion of the first transcontinental railroad. A lawless frontier outpost back then. Gunfights, murder, land grabs, mob justice, countless lynching's. Most popular saloon was appropriately named *The Bucket of Blood.*

It's a civilized little city now, and that's good news to me. I want no gunfire and lynching's to disturb my night of sleep. Check into the first motel I come across and waste no time crawling under the covers. Too drained to bother eating. Unable to write more now. Wishing for a dreamless night.

Entry 87: Cover a lot of ground today—from Laramie to Hot Springs, South Dakota—but the time passes quickly thanks to the stunning vast grasslands and no end of blue sky. A good day to be alive!

Hit the brakes when I spot the road sign.

Lost Springs, Population 4.

That warrants a look, maybe talk with someone. Find out what this town far out in the middle of nowhere, and then some, is all about.

Cross over the railroad tracks and find myself in the center of the community. Not a soul around, unfortunately. The main street (actually, there's only one street, and a very short one at that) boasts a post office, antique store, and—of all things—a bar. That explains the occupations of three of the citizens. I wonder how the fourth person in town makes a living. Mayor, possibly. Or peace officer. With no one around to chat with, I go out looking for the actual Lost Springs but, despite my best effort, they remain lost.

The Two Thousand Census put the population of Lost Springs at *one,* so there's clearly been a baby boom of late in the one hundred thirty year-old town.

Other towns out in the grasslands moved in the opposite direction and simply vanished. Seeing some of that.

Jireh, once a flourishing college town located just down the road from Lost Springs, passed into history long ago. The only evidence a living, breathing town once stood on the site is a simple roadside marker.

It tells the story of homesteaders flocking to eastern Wyoming in the early nineteen hundreds and the establishment of a religious agricultural colony and college. There was only one building to the college, but classes were offered in English, German, ethics, mathematics, art, music, psychology and, of course, the Bible.

At its height in the first decade of the twentieth century, Jireh supported a bank, two general stores, a hotel, mill, newspaper, telephone company, and garage. The good times were short-lived, however. The land was not as fertile as hoped so the farmers drifted away. The college graduated its last class in nineteen-twenty. The post office closed its doors in the middle of the Second World War, and that was pretty much it for the town.

I suspect the demise of Jireh may have been hastened

somewhat by the *Founding Fathers* rather rigid stance against fun and recreation. They not only banned alcoholic beverages, cigarettes, and gambling, but prostitution as well.

Entry 88: It's rare you'll find me mingling with the tourist hordes, but today I made an exception. I figured since I was already in the Black Hills, it would be unconscionable not to visit one of the most inspiring symbols of our democracy.

Mount Rushmore does stir emotions, no doubt about that, and one cannot help but admire the vision, bravery, attention to detail, and sheer tenacity of sculptor Gutzon Borglum and his associates. Problem I have is the viewing area is somewhat removed from the actual mountain. Drains away a bit of the impact. Also, the admission fee is quite steep and my senior park pass is not accepted, a first for that. Still, I suppose I shouldn't complain. The pass has already saved me several thousand dollars.

A group of eight Japanese schoolgirls from Nagoya ask me to snap their photos in various poses and configurations in front of the mountain (each has a camera so it is a long process), and in return they snap a few of me. We then chat for a while. Between my ten words of Japanese and their one hundred words of English, we somehow manage to *communicate*. We then part company, promising to write.

Entry 89: I'm in Hot Springs, South Dakota. A pretty town in no hurry. The old sandstone architecture is especially impressive. Big and bold buildings whose life could span the next five hundred years. Not at all what I expected to find in such an out-of-the-way place sheltered among rugged canyons and pine-covered hills.

The smiling South Asian proprietors of the *Dollar Inn at*

Battle Mountain, however, come as no surprise at all. They present me welcoming gifts of a baseball cap with the motel's name stitched above the brim, along with a leather wallet. A nice touch.

The first white settlers reached Hot Springs in the eighteen-eighties, pushed aside the Sioux, and within a few years trains were unloading passengers eager to stick a toe in the natural warm waters.

I must test the springs before I head back out on the road and begin the stretch run back home...but my thoughts are mostly elsewhere today, to a day exactly thirty-six years earlier. It's one of those anniversaries which defy the passage of time, the moment vivid in that mental diary we all carry around with us.

I'm talking about my final hours in Saigon.

I'm stretched out on the bed in the motel right now, computer in my lap, TV on in the background, working my way through a large bag of *M&M's*, trying to separate the tightly-tangled threads of that day so long ago I can write about it. Not as easy as I thought it would be.

General historical facts regarding time and place are simple enough to bring into play, but it's no piece of cake resurrecting the raw emotions long since diluted and dimmed by the passage of time. They resist being ferreted out. A likely defense mechanism and a damn effective one. The burden of carrying around the weight of every deep emotion felt over the decades would send us into a hopeless tailspin. Still, a few always manage to hang around. It's these persistent survivors which help tell the story of our time on this earth. It's an incomplete package, of course, but it's all we have and we have to make do with it.

Saigon. The date was April twenty-ninth. Pre-dawn.

My day begins with a deep *thud* rising up under me and rattling the bed, knocking me out of a deep sleep.

While I'm shaking the cobwebs from my head, the metallic thunder begins to roll in on the crest of wave after wave. A round impacts down the street. I hear glass breaking. Shouting. Fire spreads in some distant neighborhood. I can see the orange glow from the balcony. Tracer bullets arc across the sky. The earth sways, then shutters. More eruptions, now walking in my direction.

The battle for Saigon has begun. It won't be much of a battle, but we knew that already.

The Vietnamese woman climbs out of bed and calmly walks to the bathroom and closes the door behind her. I hear the shower running. I don't know her name and she doesn't know mine, and that's just fine with the two of us. These days, as cold reality crowds in close, one takes momentary refuge when and where one finds it. The more anonymous the better. Easier that way.

I do remember her telling me she had worked in a bank, but the Chinese owners had looted the vault of gold and dollars and fled to Hong Kong a few weeks earlier. I spotted her huddled in the courtyard of my building just before midnight. She'd missed the overnight curfew and took cover where she could. Not wise to chance running into a police or military patrol. Too many itchy fingers and God knows what else lurking out there in the dark.

The incoming fire eases, then fades away. I head for the kitchen to make a pot of tea. Tune in to the U.S. Armed Forces radio station. Listening for the signal to head to pre-assigned evacuation points. Bing Crosby crooning *White Christmas* is the cue the evacuation is starting.

I'm cut off from the rest of the world. International phones are down, the telex dead, so there's no way to file even a barebones story back to the States. Nothing really for me to do now other than try to mentally gear-up for the long day ahead.

Home for me the past month has been an apartment which takes up the entire second floor of an imposing three-story mansion situated on a tree-lined boulevard. It had once been the grand residence of a colonial-era French government official, but the French were long gone, and in the mid-nineteen sixties the place had been converted into luxurious apartments for Yankees with dollars.

The ceilings are high, the floors teak and tile. The louvered windows feature green shutters. Ivy creeps up the sides of the pale yellow building, and the tidy, well-tended walled garden is notable for its trio of dwarf tamarind trees and gale of bougainvillea.

It's not the type of place one would normally expect to find a junior reporter, but the city by now had pretty much emptied of wealthy foreign businessmen, so I was able to snatch up the fully-furnished apartment for a *song*.

The woman stands at the front door, heading out. I offer her my remaining Vietnamese money because I sure as hell no longer need it, but she politely declines. We wish one another good luck. She'll need it more than I do, although the day is still very young.

I jump in the shower, dress, make some breakfast, and take a cup of tea out on the balcony. Heavy clouds off to the north. Thunder. Not sure if it's natural or man-made. Two columns of smoke hang motionless in the still air over the airport a few miles away. There's no air traffic now. Fixed wing evacuation is only a memory so it's up to U.S. Marine helicopters to save our necks, if they can.

Okay, the cards have been dealt, and there's no choice but to play the hand to its inevitable conclusion. Nothing left to do now but wait for the signal to move.

From pretty much the moment I'd arrived in Saigon, the military situation was in a state of steady deterioration at all points of the compass. Still, the uncertain future, all the craziness, actually took on a normalcy of sorts after a while. We all knew the roof would soon enough be caving in on us, but we went about our jobs without high drama or undue alarm. Plenty enough time for that later.

An abrupt end to delusional spinning that things were at least halfway normal came to an abrupt end on April fourth, at four in the afternoon.

I'm sitting at my desk, smoking a cigarette, thinking about drifting over to the *Continental Hotel* across the street for an early dinner and maybe hookup with some colleagues. The day had been a long one. Hell, they were all long ones by now. Up before dawn, on the phone weaving together the divergent elements of the deteriorating military situation, no piece of cake given the drying up of credible sourcing, and the refusal of some of the top brass at the American Embassy to drop the boneheaded notion the situation was still salvageable.

While the military situation's lousy, at least the fixed-wing evacuation out of Ton Son Nhut Airport is going okay. The few remaining expatriates, their so-called dependents (often bargirls), along with endangered Vietnamese who work for, or who had worked for the American war effort in some capacity, and pretty much anyone with gold or dollars to buy their way out, are onboard U.S. military flights making their way to Clark Air Base in the Philippines.

I'm about to head out the door when I spot something out of the corner of my eye. I look out the window and there it is, looming large, lumbering along at slow speed and low altitude, moving nearly parallel to my line of sight. It's an American *C-5a Galaxy* transport. A huge aircraft.

Low-flying planes are not an unusual sight over Saigon, but this one's different. The rear door and right side rear hatch are wide open, black cavities set against the gleaming silver fuselage. I see it clearly. My heart sinks. I follow the plane until it disappears behind some buildings. Seconds pass, then a muffled *boom*. So much for dinner and whatever else diversionary I could dredge up for that night.

I'm alone in the bureau at the moment aside from two local staffers, so I take it upon myself to head out. I race down two floors to *Le Loi Street* and commandeer our secretary's motor scooter parked at the curb and soon reach a remote section of the airport fence line where I somehow manage to flag down a Vietnamese Army helicopter which ferries me to the crash site.

It's later learned the U.S.-bound, orphan-laden cargo plane was flying at an altitude of twenty thousand feet when the locks failed on the rear loading ramp, causing the door to rip open, triggering explosive decompression. The explosion severs control cables to the tail. Left only with limited control, the flight crew somehow manages a one hundred eighty degree turn and head back to Ton Son Nhut. Turning onto the final approach, the plane suddenly loses altitude and slams belly-first into a rice paddy, skids along for a while before going airborne again for a half mile or so. It then skips over the Saigon River and rams into a dike, breaking into pieces.

One hundred fifty-three people perish, including seventy-three Vietnamese orphans, most fathered by American servicemen, heading for new lives in the United States. Eighty volunteer caregivers also die, numbering many American women. Miraculously, there are survivors.

The rescue effort's well underway when I'm dropped off in the paddy. There isn't much left of the aircraft. Just twisted chunks of assorted size resting every which way in the chewed up mud and stubble.

The surrounding area's littered with toys, picture books, crib blankets, baby bottles, and infant clothing. I spot a nurse's cap, a stroller, suitcases. Disgorged seats are everywhere. Papers flutter about. I snare one in mid-air. It details the adoption of one of the young passengers. The adoptive parents live in Los Angeles.

Survivors pulled from the mangled wreckage are huddled together and being checked out by medical personal before being airlifted to the airport terminal. Some are crying, others whimper, the majority are silent, in shock, lingering beyond reach in some faraway place we all go when the present, and immediate past, are simply too painful to allow intrusion.

I walk around the wreckage, slogging through the torn up paddy. Then I see it, and wish I hadn't. A leg, a child's leg, shoeless, sticking out from under a slab of fuselage. The leg is unmarked. Not a single visible injury. The toes are still pinkish. The rest of the little body, *if* there is a rest of a body, is buried in the thick mud and fuel-coated brown water. I point out the leg to a rescuer and move on.

As the sun begins to set, I'm approached by an American man. I suspect CIA or military adviser.

"Don't you think we better get out of here?" It's more a command than a question. "This is *Charlie's* turf now and it's not a place you want to be when it gets dark."

He doesn't have to ask twice. We catch the last helicopter back to the airport terminal.

The "Orphans Crash" was the defining moment when Saigon truly broke from its past and began preparing for the future, such as it was.

Fear is metastasizing, and fast. It eradicates faith and mugs civility. A lucky few can swallow fear and get on with their day. Everyone else gags on it.

As the clock ticks down, not so many expatriates are sipping gin and tonics and afternoon tea on the veranda of the *Continental.* Ever fewer brassy and strutting streetwalkers and hustlers prowl the streets. Hotel rooms empty of aid workers and private contractors. Restaurants shut their doors. Schools close. Bureaucrats fail to show up for work. Army and police uniforms are discarded in the street by young men who wisely no longer wish to be linked with the current regime. There's a dramatic surge in street begging, crime is up, hoarding and looting intensifies. Parents hold their children closer than ever. Saigon's population doubles practically overnight as refugees flock in from the countryside, villagers mostly, wandering aimlessly about, gawking in disbelief at the crush of the big city. A few diehard South Vietnamese units are putting up a stout defense at a several points leading into Saigon, but it's just a matter of time until they're overrun.

As an American, I suppose I should feel some sense of shame at where this little country has been led all for the sake of containing communism. Maybe later, when there's the luxury of time to reflect I'll try to piece it all together in my head. Pretty much all I know for certain right then is the final page of the final act of this long-running drama is being played out on a rapidly shrinking stage, and I'm on that stage, and not at all sure of my lines.

My Bureau Chief phones to tell me he's on the way over to pick me up. Says he just spoke with someone at the embassy and was told the evacuation has been given the green light and we're to hustle on over there.

I stuff a carry-on bag with some basic items I know I'll need in the next few days: toiletries, a change of underwear and socks, a folded shirt, a carton of cigarettes. Left behind will be the two never worn safari suits I'd picked up the week before from the Indian tailor who has a shop around the corner from the bureau, along with a few gifts for family back home, including a lacquered jewelry box, a bundle of raw silk, a brass bust of Buddha, and a jade carving of an elephant.

I know it's going to be a long day and just wish there was some way I could wave a magic wand and be done with it. The danger's not really an issue, at least to me. I'm pretty much numb to that. I know there's really nothing I can do about what awaits me on the street so see no need to dwell on it. Just take basic precautionary measures and pray for luck, or possibly divine intervention, if the big guy upstairs is in a really generous mood.

The logistics of the day ahead is my primary focus. Getting from point A to point B with as little drama as possible is paramount. I've mapped it all out in my head many times, trying to anticipate the potential for deviations from my script, but concede such matters rarely go according to even the best laid plans. In the end, I would probably just have to wing it in what would be a graceless exit from this debacle.

My boss shows up and we head on out in an old *Ford Bronco.* Two miles to cover. My main concern right then is not with the North Vietnamese, but leaderless gangs of armed South Vietnamese soldiers who might welcome an opportunity for a little payback against foreigners for turning tail and running. We cross paths with two small detachments, one group leaning against a wall to a now abandoned government building, the other sitting on wrought iron chairs outside a shuttered coffee shop. I'm grateful they allow us to pass unmolested.

We reach the embassy okay and abandon the *Ford* outside the main gate. My boss tosses the car keys into a curbside sewer opening, looks at me and grins. No need to make things easy for the communist victors, we reason. Silly thing to do, maybe, but it gives us something to smile about, no small feat given the circumstances.

It's chaotic at the embassy. People ten rows deep press hard against the main gate, pleading to be let in. Others try to scale the high wall, only to be met by determined U.S. Marines holding down the fort. Some people frantically wave third country passports. Thai, Indonesian, Indian, Korean, and the like. Many Vietnamese hold up official-looking documents, hoping to convince the guardians at the gate they deserve to be allowed into the compound. Many of them had faithfully supported the war effort and are now insisting on a new life in America as promised severance pay.

Other people simply look on at the commotion. Curious Vietnamese, whole families munching on rice cakes and ice cream bars, not interested in leaving, but who'd come to the embassy just for the free show. And quite a show it was turning out to be.

I catch the eye of a Marine who motions for us to go around the corner. There we find a small wood door. I knock and a young Marine unceremoniously pulls me inside, with my boss following right behind me.

"I'm an American!" I blurt out.

"No shit! Get your asses in here!"

The unfolding scene re-defines surreal.

It's raining dollars. Clouds of them. Most are charred, some singed, all spewing out of the rooftop smokestack. The order is to leave no greenbacks for the new masters. Millions of dollars going up in smoke.

Pass some American men and women sitting in lounge chairs at the swimming pool, drinking champagne and beer and singing old tunes, acting as if they don't have a care in the world.

Heavy-duty chopping is underway on a towering century-old tamarind tree which would prevent the Marines' giant *Chinook* and *Jolly Green Giant* helicopters from landing in the embassy compound. Wood chips are flying.

The goal is to ferry large numbers of people to the Seventh Fleet waiting forty miles offshore, and to finish it up in twenty-four hours, if not sooner.

The old tree stubbornly holds on to its colonial past, but eventually succumbs to the assault, to the cheers of the small army of out-of-shape men who'd been tasked to bring it down.

I move into the embassy and take the stairs to the third floor, which commands a clear view of the madhouse below. It isn't exactly sane inside the building either. Several American diplomats, armed with hammers and baseball bats, race wildly about smashing everything in sight—communications equipment, copying machines, telephones, radios, TV's, even a picture of President Ford hanging on the wall. Little is spared.

The first *Chinook* makes a beeline for the embassy, setting down in a windstorm of kicked up newspapers, beer cans, discarded clothing, seat cushions, and anything else not nailed down. It's a snug fit. The first seventy or so wide-eyed evacuees waste no time in racing up the rear ramp and the helicopter is soon airborne again, taking aim on the South China Sea.

The helicopters begin arriving in regular intervals, but with so many people awaiting evacuation at the embassy and several other pickup points around town, it's going to be a time-consuming process, and it's pretty clear some Vietnamese will be left behind.

There's also action on the embassy rooftop helipad as little *Huey's* begin evacuating embassy personnel and anyone else around, a dozen or so at a time.

I make my way up the narrow staircase and huddle behind stacked sand bags from where a small detachment of Marines is keeping a close eye on the main boulevard leading to the embassy. It's late in the afternoon by now. Scattered small arms fire can be heard.

There's really nothing left for me to do here, so I make the decision to head for the fleet. Maybe there I can find a way to file a story and to get word to the family I'm okay.

The *Huey* hovers overhead then drops to the rooftop. I move forward, bent low, feeling the wash from the rotors parting my hair. I take a seat on the greasy floor a few feet from the pilot, a baby-faced man with steely eyes. He looks at the door gunner who flashes thumbs up. We shoot skyward, rising two hundred feet directly above the embassy roof. The pilot then lowers the nose and we tear away at high speed. I catch one final glimpse of the embassy compound where a *Jolly Green Giant's* taking on a load of people who, from my high perch, look like ants scurrying about.

Saigon quickly fades from view. Simply vanishes in the dimming light. By the time the helicopter reaches the coastline and moves out over open water, the war drums beating in my head begin to fall silent.

Entry 90: Wild burro sticks its head in my car widow and refuses to budge until fed. Friendly fellow seems to actually enjoy the kosher dill pickle, but the apple brings a light to its eyes. Expresses its appreciation by slobbering on my arm.

Lots of burros out and about today in Wind Cave National Park. Buffalo, too. Great herds of them on the plains and rolling hills, now coating with spring green.

A golden buffalo calf breaks away from the big herd and trots over to investigate this odd-looking, two-legged creature. Cozies up to me like a house cat. Enjoys having its ears rubbed and back scratched. I scamper to the far side of the *Mazda* when its mother, a molting beast the size of my car, looks up from grazing, lumbers over and nudges her naïve offspring back to her own kind, but not before giving me a hard look.

This is the day I finally decided to become a vegetarian! Been thinking about taking this momentous step for a long time. Years, actually. The decision to finally cross the line had more than a little to do with my exposure to wildlife on this trip. With one glaring exception, the animals I've met haven't seemed inclined to want to actually eat me, so I'll now return the favor. Seems a fair enough trade.

Entry 91: Winterset, Iowa. Drop by the one hundred thirty year-old *Northside Cafe* for a late lunch. Sit on the very stool Clint Eastwood occupied during filming of the diner scene in *The Bridges of Madison County.*

The lone waitress on duty says lots of tourists ask to see the stool, to sit on it, have their pictures taken sitting there. "Everyone also loves the wall in the back with all the photos and other stuff from when the movie was being shot in the restaurant," she adds. "Letter there from Clint Eastwood thanking us for our cooperation...Tourists ask me all sorts of questions: *What's Clint like? Did you see Meryl? Was I in the movie?* Things like that."

I ask what she tells them.

"I mostly pass on stuff I hear people talking about who were actually here back then. I'm from Winterset, but when the movie was being made I was five years old."

Since no one else is around, I ask the waitress to snap a photo of *me* sitting on the stool. I feel a little foolish, but what the hell. Not every day I have a chance like this. *Dirty Harry*, after all, is *my man!*

I order a bowl of soup and a *BLT*, but without the *B*. Leave a ten dollar tip.

I confess to being one of the few men who actually admit liking James Waller's book, along with the film. Maybe I was drawn in by something about the Robert Kincaid character—a wandering, rootless, solitary, rugged, handsome, engaging, romantic, sensitive, sixty-something photo-journalist. I wonder why that is...

Spent much of the day visiting the covered bridges of Madison County spread out across the impossibly fertile farmlands. The fields stretch on forever, the earth pulsating with life. Easy to see why the topsoil here is called "the black gold of Iowa."

Disappointed to learn the actual farmhouse where much of *Bridges* was filmed is no longer open to the public. Place has been vandalized. Big mess, I'm told. What's wrong with people?!

Heavy rain and all the spring mud make it a grind. The bridges are interesting enough but nothing all that special, but that reaction may have been largely influenced by the weather and all that sucking mud. I'd hoped for more visually from the bridges, but admit my expectations were probably set too high. It's also possible I've become jaded by the sheer volume of astonishing panoramas served up to me all these many months, and now require ever more and more visually to maintain my interest level. An unfortunate state of affairs to find myself in. Just hope I can muster one final burst of energy to carry me through to the end, and hopefully wrap up this road trip on a high note.

Entry 92: High note! It's John Wayne's birthday! *The Duke* was born right here in Winterset one hundred four years ago, and this All-American, *apple pie* town isn't about to let anyone forget it.

There's a big celebration underway, as there is every year at this time. Banners are strung across Main Street, the town square's decorated with flags and flowers. Lots of tourists arriving by automobile, Harley, tour bus, and horseback. There's a pancake breakfast at the fire station, a parade, and a five kilometer walk/run. The bakery's busy churning out *Duke Cupcakes*, the ingredients containing two of the things John Wayne liked most: *Tootsie Rolls* and tequila. Of course, there's no shortage of merchandise for sale every which way you look. Twenty bucks for a John Wayne *bobblehead doll.* A treasured souvenir.

Attended a screening of *"Rio Grande"* at the vintage *Iowa Theater*. The actor who played Wayne and Maureen O'Hara's son in the nineteen-fifty film was there, and is this year's honored guest in Winterset. It's the same kid who was in *The Yearling* with Gregory Peck. Claude Jarman looks pretty much the same as he did back then, only sixty-five years older.

Tonight's the fund-raising auction for the planned John Wayne Birthplace Museum. One auction *lot* caught my eye. An actual floorboard from the home of General Armstrong Custer. I may bid on it. Not everyday something like that comes along.

Wayne's daughter Aissa is also in town to assist in getting the museum up and running. Seeing her around town. Very pretty woman. Had a bit part in the movie her dad directed, *The Alamo*, when she was four.

The museum will be located close to the tiny, nicely-restored home where the biggest box office draw of all time was born. The fact his parents scooped up baby John (Marion Mitchell Morrison, actually) and moved out of state when he was only nine minutes old doesn't seem to bother anyone.

-VI-

Mile Forty Thousand, Two Hundred Eighty-Three

Entry 93: Louisville, Kentucky. A motel not far from Churchill Downs. A fierce thunderstorm is raking the city, rattling the window and flooding the parking lot. Impenetrable sheets of rain make it impossible to pick out the heavy traffic passing by on *I-64*, less than fifty yards away, but there's no muffling the roar of big rigs barreling down the highway.

Have some news. Important news as far as *I'm* concerned. There's really no compelling reason to get out of this warm bed this morning because I just made the decision to pull the plug on the road trip. That right...it's over.

Wasn't exactly sure when and where I'd make the formal call, but this morning the pieces fell into place with the realization there's simply nothing else left out there I feel an overwhelming urge to see at this very moment. Not even the *Rock and Roll Hall of Fame* in Cleveland, or the *Baseball Hall of Fame* in Cooperstown. That's pretty serious and tells me it's time to call it a day.

Must say I expected the end of the road to have more pomp and ceremony attached to it, the uncorking of a bottle of champagne at the very least, not this whimper of a demise in a lousy motel socked in by a gully-washer. Then again, I suppose this is as good a place as any to call it a day. Appropriate, actually.

Fits right in with the way I've lived my life the past year. Not all endings, after all, come wrapped in boxes with pretty bows.

Well, as it stands now just one final leg remains to get all the way back to the official starting point, and I hope to cover that ground in one fell swoop, provided I can ever convince myself to climb out of bed. I'm really not at all anxious to get out on the road today. I know from hard experience truck traffic in this weather will be brutal, and long stretches of mountain road in the Appalachians socked-in and treacherous.

That's the immediate concern. Also crowding my thoughts—where do I *go* from here? Not just tomorrow, but all the tomorrows to come. The cold reality is there's really no home to come home to, at least not in the conventional sense. My old townhouse is rented out and I haven't even started thinking about finding a new place to live. Odd I never gave serious consideration to that rather sobering reality until just now. One would think the subject would have come up at some point in the course of all my mental whittlings behind the wheel. Still, I suppose it's pretty small potatoes in the overall grand scheme of things. Not really worth fretting over. A technicality. It'll take care of itself in due course.

While I don't have a clue *where* the next chapter of my life will unfold, one thing I *do* know for certain there's simply no way I will allow myself to settle back into the old life. That would defeat the purpose of the road trip, defeat me, and I couldn't live with such a betrayal.

Maybe the smart, short-term move will be to head straight for the Virginia cabin where the journey began in earnest all those months ago. Spend a few weeks on the mountaintop in that embracing solitude. Rest the body. Regain focus. Open the mind to possibilities. Listen to the heart. Wash socks.

There are important decisions to make in the days and weeks ahead on the direction of my life from here on out, but I'm confident I'll come up with something. I always have...

And with that, this journal comes to an end.

CPSIA information can be obtained at www.ICGtesting.com
Printed in the USA
BVOW031910100413

317855BV00002B/195/P

9 781432 798024